AVKO Sequential Spelling 1 for Home Study Learning

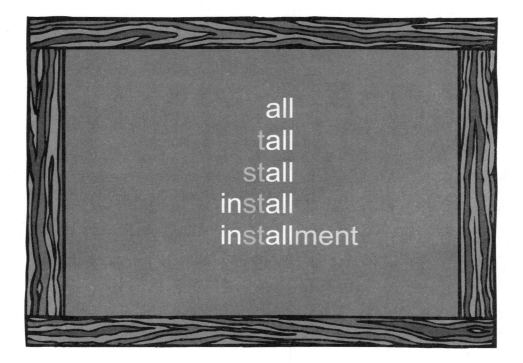

by

Don McCabe

AVKO Educational Research Foundation

Dedication

This book is dedicated to:
All the members of the AVKO Dyslexia Research Foundation,
but especially to the memory of one of its first members,

Mary Clair Scott
without whose work and devotion to the cause of literacy,
the AVKO Foundation might never have gotten off the ground,

Betty June Szilagyi
who was my first and by far my most important teacher,

Devorah Wolf
without whose encouragement and commitment
to the ideals of AVKO
this edition would not be possible,

Ann, Robert, and Linda McCabe
all of whom have sacrificed much of their time and energy
helping AVKO grow
as well as all those friends and relatives
who have been a source of encouragement.

May this book help you to help others improve their abilities to read and write.

Rev. ed. of *Sequential Spelling* ©1975 AVKO Educational Research Foundation, 3084 W. Willard Road, Suite 301, Clio, Michigan 48420
1 2 3 4 5 6 7 8 9 10 11 Printing   Year 03 93 92 89 87 85 83 81 79 76 74

Publisher's Cataloging in Publication Data

McCabe, Donald J.
     Volume 1 of an 7 Volume series. 1. Spelling—Miscellanea. 2. Reading—Miscellanea. 3. Curriculum—Miscellanea 4. Literacy and Tutor Reference Tool.
Library of Congress Subject Headings: Spelling, Curriculum
Library of Congress Classification Number: LB1050.2F79
Library of Congress Card Number: To be determined
Dewey Decimal Classification Number 428.4
ISBN: 1-56400-961-0

Telephone: (810) 686-9283 FAX: (810) 686-1101
Websites: http://www.avko.org & http://www.spelling.org
E-Mail: info@spelling.org

The Basic Concepts of Teaching Spelling by Word Families

You may have used the concept of rhyming words that have the same letter endings to help your students learn to read. For example, you may have introduced the word *at*, then also shared *cat*, *bat*, *sat*, and maybe even *scat*. Unfortunately, you have never had any source book for finding all the rhyming words with the same spelling patterns. [NOTE: In the latest academic jargon word families are now called "rimes." The consonants, consonant blends, and digraphs that precede the word family (or rime) are now called onsets. Use whatever term you wish with your students. In this book, I generally use the terms *base* or *word family* rather than the new jargon word "rime."]

The Patterns of English Spelling (formerly *Word Families Plus*) is now available to be used as a source book so that you can teach any word family. This is not just a simple collection of word lists. This book consists of complete patterns to help your students (and quite often parents and teachers!) see patterns that exist and to lock in on those patterns with their "computer" brains. For example, I believe that if you can teach your students (or anyone) the word *at*, you can also teach them:

b**at**	bats	batted	batting		
c**at**	cats				
sc**at**	scats				
fl**at**	flats	flatted	flatting		
p**at**	pats	patted	patting		
sp**at**	spats				
m**at**	mats	matted	matting		
r**at**	rats	ratted	ratting		
b**atter**	batters	battered	battering	battery	batteries
fl**atter**	flatters	flattered	flattering	flattery	
m**atter**	matters	mattered	mattering		
b**attle**	battles	battled	battling		
c**attle**					
r**attle**	rattles	rattled	rattling		

OR, for a more sophisticated example, from the word **act** you can build:

act	acts	acted	acting	active	action
f**act**	facts				
tr**act**	tracts				traction
attr**act**	attracts	attracted	attracting	attractive	attraction
distr**act**	distracts	distracted	distracting		distraction
extr**act**	extracts	extracted	extracting	extractive	extraction
subtr**act**	subtracts	subtracted	subtracting		subtraction
contr**act**	contracts	contracted	contracting		contraction

Perhaps the most important difference between the traditional approach to spelling and the AVKO (**A**udio-**V**isual-**K**inesthetic-**O**ral) approach is that we use tests as a **learning** device and **not** as a method of **evaluation**. I believe that the natural method of learning is learning from mistakes, and that is why I want children to correct their own mistakes **when** they make them—so they can learn from them.

We developed the *AVKO Sequential Spelling Tests* to utilize the word family approach sequentially and to apply the very simple techniques of having students correct their own mistakes **when** they make them—not hours, days, or even weeks later.

Use a Dry Erase Board or Something Similar to Give AVKO Sequential Spelling Tests

---

The First Day

On your first day of using Sequential Spelling, share with your students:

I have some good news and some bad news.

First the bad news: Today and every day until we finish this book, we are going to have a spelling test. The good news is that you will correct your own paper. But before we start, I want you to take out a sheet of paper and put your name on it.

Did you spell your name correctly?

Good. That's my first test.

My next test is like a doctor's test. It's not for a grade so don't worry about it. Okay? Now write the following sentence:

We are all beginning to be good spellers.

If any of your students shows signs of struggling with the sentence, just ask them to try to spell the word *beginning* only. If they still find it difficult to put down anything, ask them to just put down—in any order—some of the letters that might be in the word *beginning*.

Now collect their papers.

On the 5th day, you will be able to demonstrate that your students who couldn't spell *beginning* on the first day were able to correctly spell it without ever having seen or studied the word. And remember that according to Harry Greene's *The New Iowa Spelling Scale* (1954) only 8% of all public school 3rd graders can be expected to spell this word and just barely 60% of all public school 8th graders can spell the word *beginning*! We will expect that you will point that out to your students on the 5th day.

If your students have their own copy of the *AVKO Student Response Book for Sequential Spelling*, have them open their books to page 3. Note the location of Day 1. It is in the *middle* column of page 3. Day 2 is in the middle column on page 5. Day 3 is in the middle column on page 7. Day 4 is in the middle column on page 9, and so forth. Please note the AVKO motto on the bottom of these pages:

Mistakes are Opportunities to Learn

The reason for this arrangement is to prevent children from copying the base word that they had the day before and then just adding the -s, -ed, or -ing ending as the case may be. Just as children don't learn by copying from others, they don't learn by copying from themselves.

If you do not use the student response books, use a notebook with single sheets of paper. Use one sheet for each day's spelling lesson."

● *In the column marked 1st day/Lesson 1, please write the word "in" as in: "Come in. Come in." At least guess what letter in begins with. If you don't get it right, it's no big deal! You may erase it and write it correctly.*

After your students have attempted writing *in*, ask them what the first letter of *in* is. Hopefully they will shout out, "I!" Now, you write on the dry erase board (or something similar) just the letter "I." Now ask what the last letter of *in* is. Again, they might shout out, "N!"

On the dry erase board you now show the *-in*. (It really doesn't matter what color you use for the I and the N. I personally like to use green for the word family patterns to contrast later on with the black *beginning letters.)*

Depending upon the age of your students and their attitudes, you may try to get them to spell aloud the word with you (the oral channel) as they trace over their corrected spelling (the kinesthetic channel).

● Then give the second word, **pin** as in *"Let's play* **pin** *the tail on the donkey."* **pin**.After your students have attempted the word ***pin***, you again show the beginning *p* written in black and then the ending ***in*** written in green. They can see all three letters together that form the word ***pin***. Then add the letter *p* in front of ***in*** to make ***pin***.
● The third word is **sin** as in *"It's a* **sin** *to tell a lie"*? **sin**

Again, you should show the ***in*** in ***sin*** by having the ***in*** printed in green. Then, add the black letter ***s*** in front to change ***in*** to ***sin***.

The last word for the first day contains a consonant blend. This consonant blend may be missed by almost all your students. Don't

worry about it. Before the year is out, all your students will automatically recognize the sound of ***sp*** and write ***sp*** when they hear it.

● *The last word for today is* **spin**. *"I would like to* **spin** *the wheel on the Wheel of Fortune."* **spin**.

As you go through the procedure with **spin**, I recommend that you work through the word backwards! In other words, this time, ask what the last two letters are and then show *-in*. (On the dry erase board write ***in*** in green.) Then ask what letter comes just before the sound of ***in***. Show the ***pin*** and ask your children if they can hear the word ***pin*** in the word ***spin***. Ask for the first letter and then show **spin**. On the dry erase board just add first the ***p*** in front of ***in*** to make ***pin*** and then the ***s*** in front of ***pin*** to make ***spin***.

Now tell your students that if they have made all their corrections, they will receive a star on their paper.

If your students wrote *pins* or *sipn* for *spin* and failed to catch their mistake and correct it, you should *NOT* give them a star. I recommend you don't give them anything except encouragement that tomorrow they will have a chance to do better and get a *star*. But make sure that they correct their misspellings. Don't just put a check mark by the misspelling; have them erase *pins* or *sipn* and spell *spin* correctly.

Second Day

Have your children turn to page 5 in their *AVKO Student Response Book for Sequential Spelling,* or if you're using your own paper, have your children take out their spelling folder you had them fold the day before. If you are working with the paper, have them go to the second sheet where you had them write Lesson 2. You may begin by telling your children:

● *Today, the first word is **I**. "I like you and **I** like being your teacher."*

Ensure your students use the capital I to spell *the* word. **I**. If they spell the word **eye**, you know they have a good memory for words. Congratulate them on their great memories. Then let them know that there are sometimes different spellings for the same sound, mostly because we have different meanings sometimes for the same sound. The **eye** is what you use to see with. The word **aye** is an old fashioned way of saying yes that we still use in meetings with the expression: All in favor, say "**Aye**!" It's not necessary to teach the word **aye** right now, but I think your children will enjoy learning this word.

● The second word is **pins** as in: *"I don't like to sit on either **pins** or needles."* **pins**.

Right from the beginning I will be showing the importance of the position of letters in words. So, ask first for the last letter. If any students say "**z**", you know they have great ears. In our language we almost always use the letter **s** for the "**z**" sound when it makes a plural. We prefer that you don't bother with any formal grammatical explanation. Just have them write the **s** for the last letter. Then ask for the first letter. Most students should be able to guess that the first letter is **p** in **pins**. Now, ask what two letters go after the **p** and before the **s**. Show the word **pins**. Have your students correct their own papers. Make sure they erase any errors and spell the words correctly. Please make sure that they try. Some students are so afraid of making mistakes that they will want to wait until you have put the correct spelling on the dry erase board before they write. Please, please, please don't let them do that. They will not learn if they simply copy correct spelling. They will learn only if they attempt to spell the word and then, and only then, correct any mistakes that they make.

● The third word is **sins** as in, *"There are two kinds of **sins**: **sins** of commission (bad things we do) and **sins** of omission (good things we don't do)."* **sins**.

Ask for the last letter. Ask for the two letters in front of the final **s**. Show the combination **-ins** in green. Then ask for the first letter. Show the **s** written in black. Show the entire word **sins** with the initial **s** in black and the final **ins** in green. Remember when I say black and green, I don't really mean you must use those specific colors. You may use whatever contrasting colors you enjoy using.

● The fourth word is **spins**. *"I like the way the wheel of fortune **spins**."* **spins**.

Show the last three letters: **ins** in green. Ask what comes just before the **-ins**. Write in black the **p** that makes **pins**. Then ask for the first letter. Now show the whole word **spins**. The letters **sp** should be in black. The **ins** should be in green.

At this point, in effect, we have reviewed the four words we started with on the first day (**in**, **sin**, **pin**, **spin**) while introducing the final **-s**. Now we begin to build on the /**in**/ sound as well as to review and reinforce the **in**.

To the children you might say:

Now, I'm going to give you a really tough word. Usually, this word isn't taught until the 6th grade, but I'm sure all of you are smart enough to handle it. Okay? Ready?

● *Number 5 is **kin**. "Relatives are often called **kin**. On the news, you often hear an announcer saying that the names of the victims of an accident are being withheld pending notification of the next of kin."* **kin**. *Did everybody end the word **kin** with the word **in**?* (Write the **in** with green.)

*Good. Now, can anybody guess what letter will come just before the **in** in **kin**?*

One of your students may have put the letter **c** as the first letter. That was an intelligent mistake. Very often the /**k**/ sound is spelled with a **c** as it is in **cat**. Your students will eventually get the feel for words and know when they should use **c** and when they should use **k** for the /**k**/ sound.

● *Now we come to number 6 which is a word that usually isn't taught until the 3rd grade and that is the word* **skin**. *"Skin comes in many beautiful colors."* **skin**.

On your dry erase board you have just the -**in** in **kin** showing. Whether or not your students know the **sk** is not important at this time. You are drilling on the /**in**/ sound with real words that they could be coming into contact with in the real world. So, you show the **k** in front of **in**, making **kin** which they just had a moment ago.

Now, when you ask everybody to make sure that they have **kin** and to put one letter before the **kin** in **skin**, you should notice the excitement that is generated when your students realize that they are going to spell **skin** correctly even before you write it on the dry erase board. Number seven is a word that normally isn't taught until the 4th grade, and statistically speaking, less than half of a third grade class can spell this word,[1] but I believe all your children will be able to spell this word, if not now, then on the final test in this class.

● *Number seven is* **win**. *"Everybody loves to* **win**.*"* **win**.

Show the **in** with green. Put the **w** in black.

The last word for the day is also a word that is usually not taught until late in the 4th grade.

● *Number eight is* **twin**. *I wish I had a* **twin** *sister (or* **twin** *brother).* **twin**.

---

[1] Greene, Harry. *The New Iowa Spelling Scale*, Univ. of Iowa, 1954. This is also found in *The Reading Teachers List of over 5,500 Basic Spelling Words* published by AVKO.

Show the **in**. Then show the **win** in **twin**. Show the **tw** and then the **in**. Show **twin**.

The Third Day

We begin the third day by having your children take out their *AVKO Student Response Book for Sequential Spelling* or if you're using your own paper, have them take out their spelling folder and go to the third sheet, column one, that has been marked Lesson 3.

On this third day we will begin the slow process of teaching your children to form the ending -**ed** correctly. There is no need at this time to encumber your students' minds with rules about doubling consonants. We will simply form the habit of spelling /**ind**/ -**inned**. This way, when the rules for doubling letters are presented in their regular reading books, the students will find it easier to understand them. But, for now, please do not go into short vowels and long vowels. It's not at all necessary. In fact, it generally tends to confuse students.

You may start by saying:

● *Number 1 is* **thin**. *"My father was so* **thin***, you couldn't see him if he turned sideways."* **thin**.

First, show the -**in**; then the **th**-. If your children don't know about the letters **th** having a single sound, then now is the time to tell them. They will get plenty of practice recognizing and spelling the **th** sound. Please don't teach your children the difference between the voiced and unvoiced **th** sounds now. Just correctly pronounce the words, and they will learn to spell both **th** sounds with **th**.

● *Number 2 is* **pinned**. *"I remember getting* **pinned** *to the mat in ten seconds by a really great wrestler."* **pinned**.

Again, write the green-**in**-; then say "double the n and add ed to get –**inned**.

8

Now with your black pen write the **p-** in front to get the full word **pinned**.

● *Number 3 is* **sinned**. *"Everybody has sinned sometime."* **sinned**.

Write in green -**in**- -**inned**. **A**dd s in black in front to get **sinned**.

● *Number 4 is* **I**. *"Do* **I** *like you? Of course* **I** *do.* **I**.*"*

Write: **I**. Show that the word **I** is always capitalized. (As a bonus you might want to give them the word eye and point out that the shape of the word looks something like two eyes and a nose in the middle. And as an added bonus you can even give the word "aye" as in "Aye, aye, sir" or "All in favor say aye." You might even want to teach the opposite of aye which is nay.)

● *Number 5 is* **shin**. *"My baby brother used to kick me in the* **shin**.*"* **shin**.

Write: -**in**. Put **sh**- in front to get **shin**.

If your students haven't learned the /**sh**/ sound is made with the two letters **sh**, now is the time to tell them. They will get almost as much practice using the **sh** in their spelling as you will--keeping your children quiet when you're talking on the phone. Sh-h-h!

● *Number 6 is* **skins**. *"Fur coats are made from animal* **skins**.*"* **skins**.

Write: -**in**-. Add an **s** to get-**ins**. Put **k** in front to get –**kins**. Put **s** in front to get **skins**.

● *Number 7 is* **wins**. *"Jack* **wins** *more than he loses."* **wins**.

Write: -**in**- -**ins wins**.

● *Number 8 is* **twins**. *"There were two sets of* **twins** *in our family."* **twins**.

Write: -**in**- -**ins** -**wins twins**.

● *Number 9 is* **be**. *"I wonder what I'm going to* **be** *when I grow up."* **be**.

Write: -**e be**.

● *Number 10 is* **begin**. *"It's time to* **begin** *learning to spell."* **begin**.

Write: -**in**. Show just **be**-. Ask your students what letter should be between the **be**- and the -**in**. Then show: **begin**.

● *Number 11 is* **chin**. *"I really took it on the* **chin**.*"* **chin**.

Write: -**in ch**- **chin**.

If your students don't know that the letters **ch** have a sound of their own, the sound you hear at both the beginning and the end of the word **church**, now's the time to tell them. (When two letters have but one sound, they are called digraphs. The most common digraphs are: **th**, **ch**, and **sh**.)

● *Number 12 is* **she**. *"**She** is my best friend."* **she**.

Write: -**e sh**- **she**.

The Fourth Day

The fourth day we begin by opening to page 9 in your students' *AVKO Student Response Book for Sequential Spelling,* or by having them go to the fourth sheet in their spelling folder where the first column will be labeled Lesson 4.

Give the following words in sentences as shown or make up your own sentences. Remember, after each word is given, you should write the word correctly on your dry erase board and let your students immediately correct any mistakes that they might have made. You might want to continue using contrasting colors to help your students recognize the patterns that are in the words. For example, when you give the correct spelling of spinning, you might first write using green the base **in**. Then "double the **n**" and add **ing** to get **inning**. Then put a black **p** in front of **inning** to get **pinning** and then a black **s** to get **spinning**.

1. **thins** A painter sometimes **thins** his paint with turpentine. **thins**

2. **pinning** Are you good at **pinning** a tail on a donkey? **pinning**

3. **sinning** Is it a sin to misspell **sinning**? **sinning**

4. **spinning** Have you ever seen a **spinning** wheel? **spinning**

5. **shins** It's no fun to get kicked in the **shins**. **shins**

6. **skinned** Trappers **skinned** the animals for their furs. **skinned**

7. **winning** I enjoy **winning** a lot more than I do losing. **winning**

8. **inner** Your **inner** voice that tells you right from wrong. **inner**

9. **be** I wish you would **be** more careful **be**

10. **begins** I hope this **begins** to make some sense to you. **begins**

11. **chins** When Jim is in the gym, he **chins** himself 10 times. **chins**

12. **we** Do we know where **we** are going? **we**

13. **bee** It's no fun to be stung by a **bee**. **bee**

14. **see** What do you **see** when you close your eyes? **see**

15. **tree** Did George Washington chop down a cherry **tree**? **tree**

Now is a good time to talk about homophones, words that sound exactly alike but have different meanings as well as different spellings.

in / inn We found an **inn** and went **in** to have a meal.

I / eye / aye **I** got a black **eye** because I forgot to say, "**Aye, aye**, sir" to the captain.

be / bee / Bea Could it **be** that Aunt **Bea** was stung by a **bee**?

we / wee/ oui **We** heard a **wee** French lad answer yes by saying, "**Oui, oui**, madame."

see / sea / si Can you **see** the **sea** from the window? **Si, si**, señor.

In some cases, words sound the same due to a dialect, such as a Southern dialect:

pin / pen You use a pin to hold things. You use a pen to write with. Pigs are kept in a pen. You can wear a pin.

The Fifth Day

On the fifth day we begin with Lesson 5.

Give the following words in sentences as shown or make up your own sentences. Remember, after each word is given, you should write the word correctly on your dry erase board and let your students immediately correct any mistake that they might have made.

1. **thinned** We **thinned** the carrots and the beets for grandpa. **thinned**

2. **thinner** Jack Sprat was quite a bit **thinner** than his wife. **thinner**

3. **sinner** If you've never committed a sin, can you be a **sinner**? s**inner**

4. **spinner** I put a little **spinner** above my hook when I go fishing. **spinner**

5. **fins** Fish have **fins** instead of legs. **fins**

6. **Mr. Skinner** Hey, mister! Have you seen **Mr. Skinner**? **Mr. Skinner**

7. **winner** You're a **winner** and not a loser. **winner**

8. **be** What do you want to **be** when you grow up? **be**

9. **inning** How many outs in an **inning**? (6! 3 for each side) **inning**

Before giving the correct spelling of beginning, check your students' papers to see if they have learned to spell this word.

Almost all students should have spelled *beginning* correctly. Now, compare this spelling to the misspellings you collected on the first day. You may share with our students how proud you are of them. They have learned a difficult word without ever having studied the word, just by paying attention and by correcting their mistakes. They are learning a great deal.

10. **beginning Shall we start all over from the beginning? beginning**

11. **chinned** Jim **chinned** himself ten times in the gym. **chinned**

12. **we We** should always try our best to be good. **we**

13. **wee** The wee little lad has an eye for **wee** little lasses. **wee**

14. **bee** Have you ever been stung by a **bee**? **bee**

15. **see** What do you **see** outside your window? **see**

16. **trees** Lumberjacks cut down **trees** to make lumber. **trees**

17. **free** Who said, "**Free** at last"? **free**

18. **agree** I **agree** with you. **agree**

19. **disagree** I hope you don't **disagree** with me. **disagree**

20. **fees** We had to pay all kinds of different **fees**. **fees**

The Sixth Day

On the sixth day we begin Lesson 6.

Give the following words in sentences as shown or make up your own sentences. Remember, after each word is given, you should write the word correctly on your dry erase board and let your students immediately correct any mistakes that they might have made.

1. **thinning** My uncle's hair is really **thinning** on top. He's almost bald. **thinning**

2. **thinnest** My Aunt Bea is the **thinnest** woman I have ever met. **thinnest**

3. **sinners** We all are **sinners**. Some more than others. **sinners**

4. **spinners** When I go fishing I bring along some special **spinners**. **spinners**

5. **tin** Have you ever heard of a cat on a hot **tin** roof? **tin**

6. **Skinner's inn** Has anybody been in **Skinner's Inn**? **Skinner's Inn**

7. **winners** I like games in which there are a lot of **winners**. **winners**

8. **inner** Your **inner** ear is very important for your balance. **inner**

9. **bee** Anything sweet will attract a **bee**. **bee**

10. **beginnings** I really enjoy new **beginnings**. **beginnings**

11. **chinning Chinning** yourself is good exercise if you can do it. **chinning**

12. **wee Wee** means small. Leprechauns are called the **wee** folk. **wee**

13. **we** Today, **we** know that leprechauns really don't exist. **we**

14. **be** If you will **be** good, you might get a surprise. **be**

15. **seen** Is it true that children should be **seen** and not heard? **seen**

16. **treed** The hounds **treed** the raccoon. **treed**

17. **frees** A governor sometimes **frees** persons wrongfully committed. **frees**

18. **agrees** Nearly everyone **agrees** with you. Salt water is hard to freeze. **agrees**

19. **disagrees** Nobody **disagrees** with their boss. Well, almost nobody. **disagrees**

20. **flee** To run away is to **flee**. Can a flea **flee**? **flee**

Note: Your language books give explanations and rules about apostrophes. You don't need to interrupt the giving of the spelling words to give an explanation. All through this series of Sequential Spelling the -'s form is used with a word following it. The students' "computer" brains will be properly programmed without rules. However, if either you or your students want the rules, freely share them.

The Seventh Day

On the seventh day we begin Lesson 7.

Give the following words in sentences as shown or make up your own sentences. Remember, after each word is given, you should write the word correctly on your dry erase board and let your students immediately correct any mistake that they might have made.

1. **bin** A **bin** is a place to store things. We used to have a coal bin. **bin**

2. **in** Welcome. Come on **in. in**

3. **inn** There's an **inn** across the street that serves really good food. **inn**

4. **spin** I love to watch figure skaters especially when they **spin** around. **spin**

5. **tins** We try to recycle all our **tins. tins**

6. **skinny** Jack Sprat was a really **skinny** man. **skinny**

7. **winning** I enjoy **winning** much more than losing. **winning**

8. **be** I would **be** really surprised if you missed this word. **be**

9. **inner** Do you know who belongs to the **inner** circle? **inner**

10. **beginner** Can you find the word inner in the word **beginner**? **beginner**

11. **chin** I think a dimple in the **chin** is rather cute. **chin**

12. **wee** Do you know what the **wee** hours of the morning are? **wee**

13. **we We** should have been in bed long before midnight. **we**

14. **bee** Some people are allergic to **bee** stings. **bee**

15. **seeing** Thomas believed that **seeing** is believing. **seeing**

16. **treeing** The dogs were **treeing** two little squirrels. **treeing**

17. **freed** Do you know when Lincoln **freed** the slaves? **freed**

18. **agreed** For once, everybody in our family **agreed** with me. **agreed**

19. **disagreed** I don't know why everybody **disagreed** with me just now. **disagreed**

20. **flees** If a flea runs away, the flea **flees. flees**

After the Eighth Day

After the eighth day, I include a 25 word spelling test. Some days the tests are easier than others, but don't panic on days like the 126th day when the word *arrangements* is presented.

REMEMBER: My learning philosophy (AVKO) is *not* concerned about teaching the spelling of any one word *per se*. I am concerned with the teaching of basic sounds for both spelling and reading. In the case of words like *range, ranges, arrange, arranges, arrangement, arrangements*, I feel that teaching the *-ange* ending, the plural ending and the suffix *–ment,* as well as the initial consonant sounds and consonant blends, is important.

REMEMBER: Encourage *speed* your students to *speed* through these tests. Give the word. Put it in a sentence. Say the word. Spell the word. Have the students (if you can) trace the corrected spelling as they spell it aloud in group chorus. Go on to the next —but make sure your students make an attempt at the spelling *before* you give the correct spelling. **Copying** your spelling does **not** help them learn. **Correcting** their own misspelling **does**.

Immediate Feedback

The most common mistake made in administering the *AVKO Sequential Spelling Tests* is to give the entire test and then correct. This method just **won't** work.

● Give each word separately.

● Say the word. Give it in a sentence.

● Let the students attempt the spelling.

● Give the correct spelling. Let students correct their mistakes.

● Then give the next word. Repeat the process of immediate student self-correction.

Grading

If you desire to give grades for spelling, I would recommend that you give tests for grading purposes separately. You may then grade your students on their learning of the spelling of the sounds—not the words. Sequential Spelling gives permission for parents (and teachers) to duplicate (for their students only) the tests that come after the 40th, 80th, 120th, 160th and 180th days. Read the sentences to your students. All they have to do is fill in the blanks. Notice that you are not testing on the whole word. You are testing only on the spelling patterns taught. (That is why the initial consonants or blends are given to the student.) NOTE: You can use these as a pre-tests, as well as post-tests, to show progress. How you grade these tests is up to you. I recommend that 0-2 wrong = A, 3-4 = B, 5-6 = C, and 7-8 = D.

If your students get more than 8 wrong, I recommend going back over the process to help them learn what they are missing.

Questions most frequently asked concerning Sequential Spelling

1. What are those asterisks (*) and exclamation marks doing next to some words?

The asterisks merely serve as a reminder to the parent/teacher that the word so marked has a **homophone** (same pronunciation, different spelling), has a **heteronym** (same spelling, different word and different pronunciation), or does not follow the normal pattern. For example, *gyp* ** should logically be spelled "*jip*."But instead of *j* we use the letter "*g.*" Instead of *i* the letter *y* is used. Likewise, the word *proper* ** should logically be spelled "*propper*"just like *hopper*, and *copper*, and *stopper*, but it isn't.

2. Why don't the words used follow grade levels? For example, _Scatter_ is a _7th_ grade word in many school's regular spelling texts.

Regular spelling texts, as a general rule, pick grade levels for words according to when the words first begin to occur in the curriculum. This would seem to make sense, but it does bring about some rather odd sequences. Since the word *ice* may not occur in the curriculum until the fourth grade (when it appears in the science class), its introduction is delayed until that time even though *nice* may occur in the first grade, *twice* in the second grade, *price* in the fifth, and *rice* in the sixth.

We believe in teaching the phonics necessary for decoding through the back door of spelling and without preaching rules that may or may not be useful. We teach the word *scatter* only after the *-at* sound has been taught in 30 different words. After the *-atter* sound has occurred in eight words, and directly after the initial *c* in *cat* and the consonant blend *sc* in *scat*, then we teach *scatter*.

3. Why do you have so many words that are outside the vocabulary of

normal adults, such as the word "tat"?

We don't believe it hurts anyone to learn a new word—but that is not why we use it. We use the word *tat* as an added practice in sounding out spellings of words having the initial /t/ sound and practice in spelling the ending -*at*. It also gives the student a pleasant surprise and ego boost when he discovers he can spell a word that he believes he has never heard nor seen before—just because he knows how to spell the sounds.

4. Should I count off for sloppy handwriting?

Since the students get to correct their own spelling, they should be expected to write clearly and legibly. In fact, I recommend that these sequential spelling tests be used for handwriting practice because the patterns, being repetitive, can be a help in developing legible handwriting. I further recommend that if your students print, that they use D'Nealian® manuscript. If your students write, we strongly recommend D'Nealian® cursive. Another excellent system is the Italic by Getty-Dubay. But whatever system you use, we believe that **writing must be legible**. So, yes, by all means, take off for sloppy handwriting (provided the student has no physical disability and has sufficient small motor skills to write legibly).

5. Do I have to use all the words that are in the tests? Can I drop some? Can I change some?

No, you don't have to use them all. You can drop some. You know your children better than I do. Yes, you can substitute other words for the ones I have selected. *The Patterns of English Spelling* is your best reference to select from. If, for example, you would rather start with the -at, bat, rat, cat, sat family, be my guest. You can use your pencil to write in your choices. Every student is different. Don't be afraid to trust your own judgment.

6. Can I give the same test more than once during the day?

Yes. If your students can profit from that, fine. I recommend, however, that you allow a minimum of two hours to pass between re-tests.

I also recommend four as the absolute maximum number of times that Sequential Spelling be given in one day, whether repeats or new lessons.

7. I have a child who is a 5th grader. May I use Sequential Spelling 1 to start one hour, Sequential Spelling 2 to start the 2nd hour, 3 for the third, etc.? I want my child to become as good a reader and speller as possible.

Why not? If it works, it works. If it doesn't, then try something else. You could try going through four days of Sequential Spelling I every day until it is finished and then move through four days of Sequential Spelling II every day, and continue on through four levels of Sequential Spelling in one year.

8. Why are some words in bold print?

The words in **bold print** are those that are the most commonly used words and the most important to learn. You will also notice that some words (like the word **doesn't**) that don't follow regular patterns are repeated many times throughout the series. If your students learn to spell any of the words that are not in bold face, that is a bonus. What I want the students to learn is to spell the most common words and to learn the most common patterns that occur in words. You will discover that most of these patterns consist of only two, three, or four letters. A big word like *misunderstandings* can be broken into the following patterns: *mis/un/der/st/and/ing/s*.

9. Do I have to teach all the homophones and homographs listed?

Absolutely not. I have listed them for your convenience. If you wish to teach them, fine. If you don't, fine. I only ask that when they come up that you definitely use the word in a sentence that helps the student pick the right word. For example: Don't just say **billed**. The students may think about the word **build**. Instead, say something like: "**billed**. *We were* **billed** *for extra carpeting.* **billed**.*"

10. What does TPES stand for at the bottom of the pages?

TPES stands for *The Patterns of English Spelling*. This book contains all the words that share a common spelling pattern placed on the same page (or pages in the case of families like the -tion family). In our Sequential Spelling Series, I list most of the words in each family, but not all. If a parent/teacher wants to include more or wants to give special assignments to the gifted students, I have included the page references. This book may be purchased from the AVKO Educational Research Foundation, 3084 W. Willard Rd., Clio, MI 48420. For more information call toll free: 1-866-AVKO 612.

11. Can I use the words in Sequential Spelling for composition?

Yes, of course. Having your students create sentences out of the words is good exercise for their minds and will allow you to determine if they truly understand what the words really mean. You may also have them write the entire sentence that you dictate. That will help you help them handle the problems created by speech patterns, such as the "wanna" instead of "want to" and the "whacha gonna" for "what are you going to," etc. As the parent/teacher, you know your students and how many sentences they can handle as homework. You might even want to set time limits such as: Write as many sentences using today's spelling words as you can in 10 minutes.

12. Is there anything I can use to help my students' reading that will also reinforce the spelling?

AVKO's *New Word Families in Sentence Context* may be used in conjunction with Sequential Spelling. The page number given for *The Patterns of English Spelling* (TPES) also works for the *Word Families in Sentence Context*. This book may also be obtained from the AVKO Educational Research Foundation.

	1st day	2nd day	3rd day	4th day
1.	* **in**	* **I**	thin	thins
2.	** **pin**	pins	pinned	pinning
3.	sin	sins	sinned	sinning
4.	spin	spins	**I**	spinning
5.		kin	shin	shins
6.		skin	skins	skinned
7.		win	wins	winning
8.		twin	twins	inner
9.			* **be**	* **be**
10.			begin	begins
11.			chin	chins
12.			she	* **we**
13.				* **wee**
14.				* **bee**
15.				* **see**
16.				tree

* Homophones:

in	Come on in.
inn.	They spent the weekend at a country inn.
I	I really love chocolate.
eye	My brother got a black eye.
aye	All in favor, say, "Aye!"
be	We will all be there.
bee	I hate to be stung by a bee.
Bea	My Aunt Bea had a party.
we	We all went to her party.
wee	She called the baby boy a wee lad and the girl a wee lass.
oui	The French say "oui" for yes.
see	I can see you.
sea	A sea is bigger than a lake; smaller than an ocean.
si	In Spanish, the word for *yes* is *si*.

**	In *some* dialects: pin/pen.
pin	You pin the tail on the donkey. Pins and needles.
pen	You keep pigs in a pig pen. You write with a pen.

The complete -in family is found on p. 123 in *The Patterns of English Spelling* (TPES); the -inner family on p. 635; the -e & -ee families on pp. 304-305.

	5th day	6th day	7th day	8th day
1.	thinned	thinning	thin	thinner
2.	thinner	thinnest	* in	ins
3.	sinner	sinners	* inn	inns
4.	spinner	spinners	spin	spinning
5.	fins	tin	tins	tin
6.	Mr. Skinner	Mr. Skinner's	skinny	skins
7.	winner	winners	winning	winner
8.	* be	* bee	* be	* be
9.	inning	innings	inner	being
10.	**beginning**	beginnings	beginner	beginners
11.	chinned	chinning	chin	chins
12.	* we	* wee	* wee	* we
13.	* wee	* we	* we	* wee
14.	* bee	* bees	* bee	**bees**
15.	* see	* sees	seeing	* see
16.	trees	treed	treeing	trees
17.	free	* frees	freed	freeing
18.	agree	agrees	agreed	agreeing
19.	disagree	disagrees	disagreed	disagreeing
20.	fees	* flee	* flees	fleeing

* Homophones:

sees	She sees everything that happens in our neighborhood.
seas	Lakes are smaller than seas. Oceans are bigger.
seize	The police wanted to seize my uncle's car.
flee	To flee is to run away.
flea	A flea is a little insect that lives on animals.
flees	A flea flees from insecticide.
fleas	Fleas flee from insecticide.
levy/levee	The state decided to levy a tax to pay for the building of a levee.
frees	A robot frees a worker from working.
freeze	Water will freeze if it's below zero outside.

The complete -in family is found on p. 123 in *The Patterns of English Spelling* (TPES), the -inner family on p. 635, the -e & -ee families on pp. 304-305, and the -inny skinny & innie Minnie family on p 704.

	9th day	10th day	11th day	12th day
1.	**up**	ups	up	ups
2.	**cup**	cups	cupped	cupping
3.	**pup**	pups	**puppy**	my puppy's eye
4.	sup	sups	supped	supping
5.	**good**	goods	goody	good
6.	* **wood**	woods	wooded	wooden
7.	**stood**	stood	stood	stood
8.	**could**	could	could	could
9.	* **would**	**would**	**would**	**would**
10.	**food**	**wouldn't**	food	**wouldn't**
11.	* **mood**	moods	mood	moods
12.	* **brood**	broods	brooded	brooding
13.	**out**	outs	outing	outing
14.	shout	shouts	shouted	shouting
15.	bout	bouts	**about**	about
16.	lout	louts	stout	stout
17.	clout	clouts	clouted	clouting
18.	flout	flouts	flouted	flouting
19.	pout	pouts	pouted	pouting
20.	spout	spouts	spouted	spouting
21.	* **rout**	**routs**	**routed**	**routing**
22.	grout	about	**wouldn't**	**shouldn't**
23.	** **route**	**routes**	**routed**	**routing**
24.	**should**	**shouldn't**	**couldn't**	**couldn't**
25	eye	eyes	eye	eyes

* Homophones:

wood	Do you ever knock on wood? Wood comes from trees.
would	Would you please come here?
wooden	Have you ever used a wooden spoon?
wouldn't	I wouldn't do that if I were you.
mood	Are you in a good mood?
mooed	The cows mooed in the meadow.
brood	To brood is to pout.
brewed	A brew such as beer is brewed in a brewery.

The complete -up family is found on p. 130 in *The Patterns of English Spelling* (TPES); the -ood, wood & -ood food families on p. 404; the -ould family on p. 405; -out; p. 431.

	13th day	14th day	15th day	16th day
1.	upper	**up**	ups	upper
2.	Mr. Cuppy	Mr. Cuppy's	Mr. Tupper	Mr. Tupper's
3.	puppies	puppy's	puppies	puppy's
4.	**supper**	suppers	supper	suppers
5.	**good**	goodness	good	goodness
6.	* **wood**	woods	wooden	woods
7.	**stood**	stood	stood	stood
8.	**could**	**couldn't**	**could**	**couldn't**
9.	* **would**	* **wouldn't**	**would**	* **wouldn't**
10.	**food**	about	food	about
11.	* **mood**	moods	* **eye**	* **eyes**
12.	* **brood**	broods	brooded	brooding
13.	scout	scouts	scouted	scouting
14.	trout	snout	snouts	gout
15.	stout	stouter	stoutest	stout
16.	**an**	* **eye**	* **aye**	* **ayes**
17.	**can**	cans	canned	canning
18.	scan	scans	scanned	scanning
19.	**man**	man's	manned	manning
20.	* **manner**	**manners**	**manner**	**manners**
21.	**ran**	more * **than**	**bigger** than	ran
22.	bran	Nan	Nan's man	* Fran's a man
23.	thinner than	Jan	Jan's a man	Fran's man
24.	and then	stouter than	and then	moodier than
25.	moody	moodier than	moody	moodiest

* Homophones:

wood / would	The box was made out of wood. Would you please follow directions?
wouldn't / wooden	Wouldn't you know, Long John Silver had a wooden leg.
mooed / mood	The cow mooed because she was in the mood to be milked.
brood / brewed	The hen watched over her brood as the pilgrims brewed their own beer.
eye / aye / I	Will you keep an eye out for Mr. Johnson? Aye, aye, sir. I sure will.
than / then	Tom is taller than Jim. So I picked Tom and then I picked Jim.
manner/manor	In a manner of speaking, a manor is a plantation.
Francis/Frances	The name Fran is often used as a nickname for both Francis (male) and Frances (female

* Tricky Words:

super	Wouldn't it be super to be Superman?
supper	The rich have dinner. We eat supper.

The complete -an family is found on p. 121 in *The Patterns of English Spelling* (TPES); -en, p. 122, -ool p.414.

	17th day	18th day	19th day	20th day
1.	**ten**	tens	tenth	tenth
2.	**men**	men's	Amen	Len
3.	**man**	men	woman	woman
4.	**woman**	**women**	women's	women
5.	* **pen**	pens	penned	penning
6.	hen	hens	Ken	Ken's
7.	Ben	Ben's	**when**	* **then**
8.	den	dens	yen	Jen
9.	Jen	Jenny	Jenny's pen	Benny
10.	and * **then**	penny	pennies	Penny's pen
11.	wren	wrens	Glen	Glen's pen
12.	**cool**	cools	cooled	cooling
13.	fool	fools	fooled	fooling
14.	cooler than	coolest	coolers	**coolly**
15.	**plan**	plans	planned	planning
16.	pan	pans	panned	panning
17.	span	spans	spanned	spanning
18.	tan	tans	tanned	tanning
19.	Stan	Stan's pan	Dan	Dan's van
20.	van	vans	Van	Van's pans
21.	clan	clans	was	wasn't
22.	would	wouldn't	could	couldn't
23.	should	shouldn't	should	shouldn't
24.	eye	eyes	aye	ayes
25.	could	couldn't	wouldn't	would

* Homophones:

pen	Do you have a pen or a pencil?
pin	Do you have a safety pin?

than	Jack is older than Don.
then	Then what happened?

See the complete -an family on p. 121 in *The Patterns of English Spelling* (TPES); -en, p. 122; the --ool p. 414.

	21st day	22nd day	23rd day	24th day
1.	**at**	hat	hats	hatter
2.	bat	bats	batted	batting
3.	rat	rats	ratted	ratting
4.	brat	brats	pat	pats
5.	fat	fats	spat	spats
6.	flat	flats	flatter	flatters
7.	**it**	* **its** leg	* **it's too bad**	**its** ear
8.	**sit**	sits	sat	sitting
9.	pit	pits	pitted	pitting
10.	spit	spits	spat	spitting
11.	lit	slit	fit	fits
12.	split	splits	split	splitting
13.	**bit**	bits	bitten	skit
14.	pool	pools	pooled	pooling
15.	spool	spools	spooled	spooling
16.	tool	tools	cooler	coolers
17.	stool	stools	* **coolly**	* **coolly**
18.	drool	drools	drooled	drooling
19.	**school**	schools	schooled	schooling
20.	**open**	opens	opened	opening
21.	opener	openers	can opener	can openers
22.	cooler than	and then	be quiet	be quiet
23.	fit	fits	fitted	fitting
24.	flit	flits	flitted	flitting
25.	quit it	quits	quitter	quitting

* Homophones:

its	The cat bit its tongue. (its = his/her)
it's	It's too bad that it happened. (it's = it is)
coolly	She very coolly said, "Good-bye."
coolie	The Chinese coolie was practically a slave.
to/too/two	It's too bad the two boys went to school two hours too early and still were tardy, too.

See the complete -en family on p. 122 in *The Patterns of English Spelling* (TPES); the -ool, p. 414; the -at, p. 131, the -it, p. 133.

	25th day	26th day	27th day	28th day
1.	hatters	drat	drats	spat
2.	batter	batters	battered	battering
3.	**cat**	cats	battery	batteries
4.	patted	patting	Patty	Patty's hat
5.	scat	scats	mat	mats
6.	flattered	flattering	flattery	flattery
7.	scatter	scatters	scattered	scattering
8.	sitter	sitters	does	doesn't
9.	kit	kits	kitten	kittens
10.	skit	skits	kitty	kitties
11.	knit	knits	knitted	knitting
12.	wit	wits	outwit	outwitted
13.	**old**	older	oldest	quitter
14.	*** hold**	holds	held	holding
15.	**cold**	colds	colder	coldest
16.	fold	folds	folded	folding
17.	unfold	unfolded	folder	unfolding
18.	weld	welds	welded	welding
19.	meld	welded	welder	melding
20.	elder	elders	eldest	welders
21.	rattle	rattles	rattled	rattling
22.	battle	battles	battled	battling
23.	cattle	little	skittles	! "vittles"
24.	swat	swats	swatted	swatter
25.	water	waters	watered	watering

* Homophones:

hold	Will you hold my putter for me?
holed	Tiger Woods holed a twenty foot putt.

! The correct spelling of "vittles" is really *victuals*.
See the complete -atter and -itter families on pp. 637, 638 in *The Patterns of English Spelling* (TPES); the -at, p. 131; the -old, p. 241; the -eld, p. 240; the -ttle p. 603. See p. 504 for the wa- words such as water, was, watch etc.

	29th day	30th day	31st day	32nd day
1.	spats	slat	slats	chatty Patty
2.	chat	chats	chatted	chatting
3.	spatter	spatters	spattered	spattering
4.	platter	platters	**that**	**that's too bad**
5.	splatter	splatters	splattered	splattering
6.	**matter**	matters	mattered	mattering
7.	chatter	chatters	chattered	chattering
8.	shatter	shatters	shattered	shattering
9.	admit	admits	admitted	admitting
10.	permit	permits	permitted	permitting
11.	commit	commits	committed	committing
12.	omit	omits	omitted	omitting
13.	emit	emits	emitted	emitting
14.	submit	submits	submitted	submitting
15.	uphold	upholds	upheld	upholding
16.	withhold	withholds	withheld	withholding
17.	behold	beholds	beheld	beholding
18.	**gold**	golden	**sold**	unsold
19.	*** told**	untold	retold	**wasn't**
20Am.	*** mold**	molds	molded	molding
20Br.	*** mould**	moulds	moulded	moldy/mouldy
21.	**shoulder**	shoulders	shouldered	shouldering
22.	*** boulder**	boulders	*** bold**	*** bolder**
23.	litter	litters	littered	littering
24.	glitter	glitters	glittered	glittering
25.	sitter	sitters	bitter	bitterly

* Homophones:

told	Who told you that story?
tolled	The church bell tolled twelve times.
mold	Penicillin comes from mold. American Spelling
mould	Penicillin comes from mould. British Spelling.
bold	Be brave. Be bold.
bowled	The bowler bowled a perfect game.
bolder	As I grew older, I became bolder and tried a lot of new things.
boulder	It's awfully hard to shoulder a boulder.

See the complete -atter family on p. 637 in *The Patterns of English Spelling* (TPES); the -at, p. 131; the -old, p. 241.

	33rd day	34th day	35th day	36th day
1.	bet	bets	Betty	better
2.	**let**	lets	letting	letter
3.	set	sets	setting	setter
4.	sunset	sunsets	vet	vets
5.	upset	upsets	upsetting	yet
6.	**wet**	wets	wetting	let's go
7.	jet	jets	jetted	jetting
8.	pot	pots	potty	potting soil
9.	spot	spots	spotted	spotting
10.	**lot**	lots	*** a lot**	a lot of
11.	*** allot**	allots	allotted	allotting
12.	slot	slots	slotted	slotting
13.	clot	clots	clotted	clotting
14.	plot	plots	plotted	plotting
15.	blot	blots	blotted	blotting
16.	mild	milder	mildest	mild
17.	**wild**	wildly	wilder	wildest
18.	**child**	a child's toy	children	children's toys
19.	*** build**	builds	built	building
20.	*** bald**	scald	scalded	scalding
21.	settle	settles	settled	settling
22.	kettle	kettles	potter	pottery
23.	bottle	bottles	bottled	bottling
24.	water	waters	watered	watering
25.	shouldn't	couldn't	wouldn't	eyes

* Homophones:

a lot	We have a lot of fun. In fact, *an* awful *lot* of fun. See Note:
allot	How much money does the government allot for defense?
build	The Smiths want to build a new house.
billed	The Smiths were billed twice for the same item.
bald / bawled	Some men get bald. Some men get bawled out.
balled	Who took that paper and balled it up?

Note: A lot of people spell a lot as one word alot. The fact that we can put awful between a(n) and lot demonstrates that a lot is a two word expression.

The complete -et family is found on p. 132 in *The Patterns of English Spelling* (TPES); the -ot, p. 134; the -ild & -ald on p. 240.

	37th day	38th day	39th day	40th day
1.	pet	pets	petted	petting
2.	fret	frets	fretted	fretting
3.	**get**	gets	got	getting
4.	forget	forgets	forgot	forgetting
5.	net	nets	netted	netting
6.	be **quiet**	quiets	quieted	quieting
7.	cot	cots	cotter pin	cotton
8.	**hot**	hotter than	hottest	hotly
9.	jot	jots	jotted	jotting
10.	shot	shots	tot	tots
11.	* **not**	cannot	can't	cannot
12.	* **knot**	knots	knotted	knotting
13.	dot	dots	dotted	dotting
14.	rot	rots	rotted	rotting
15.	trot	trots	trotted	trotting
16.	blood	bloody	bloodier	bloodiest
17.	flood	floods	flooded	flooding
18.	**love**	loves	loved	loving
19.	glove	gloves	gloved	lovely
20.	shove	shoves	shoved	shoving
21.	a lovely * **dove**	lovely doves	lovely	lovingly
22.	prettier	prettiest	lover	pretty
23.	lover	lovers	lovelier	loveliest
24.	should	could	would	eyes
25.	couldn't	wouldn't	shouldn't	ayes

Heteronyms: dove "duv" a bird / dove "dOH'v, a past tense of dive. The other is dived.
Both are standard usage. Purists prefer dived to dove.

dove (duv)   I would love to have a dove.
dove (doh'v)   By Jove, the pirate dove into the cove.
   When the cops arrived, under the bed he dived.

* Homophones:
not   I wish you would not make so much noise.
knot   Can you untie this knot for me?

The complete -et family is found on p. 132 in *The Patterns of English Spelling* (TPES); the -ot, p. 134; the -ild, -eld, & -ald on p. 240; the -ood, p. 404; the -ove, p. 326.

Evaluation Test #1 (After 40 Days)

		Pattern being tested	Lesson word is in
1.	The lady next door just had tw**ins**.	ins	3
2.	Let's start at the beg**inning**.	inning	5
3.	He planted pine tr**ees** in his back yard.	ees	5
4.	A w**inner** never quits.	inner	8
5.	My friend w**ould** always listen to me.	ould	9
6.	He never just talks. He sh**outs**.	outs	10
7.	He eats one lunch and two s**uppers**.	uppers	16
8.	He counted to t**en** on his toes.	en	17
9.	She pl**anned** a special dinner for him.	anned	19
10.	Please stop f**ooling** around.	ooling	20
11.	The clown fell fl**at** on his face.	at	21
12.	I was f**it** to be tied.	it	23
13.	That dress fl**atters** her.	atters	24
14.	I have a spl**itting** headache.	itting	24
15.	I am forever f**olding** laundry.	olding	28
16.	I can't believe he was perm**itted** to do that.	itted	31
17.	I hope you're not ups**et** with me.	et	33
18.	Always be careful around a w**ild** animal.	ild	33
19.	It's not funny when someone sh**oves** you around.	oves	38
20.	I'm sorry I forg**ot** to say, "I'm sorry."	ot	39

I don't believe an evaluation test is necessary at this point, but just in case you think your students need an evaluation test, here it is. Use it, make your own, or just skip it.

Name_____Date_____

Evaluation Test #1

1. The lady next door just had tw_____.

2. Let's start at the beg_____.

3. He planted pine tr_____ in his back yard.

4. A w_____ never quits.

5. My friend w_____ always listen to me.

6. He never just talks. He sh_____.

7. He eats one lunch and two s_____.

8. He counted to t_____ on his toes.

9. She pl_____ a special dinner for him.

10. Please stop f_____ around.

11. The clown fell fl_____ on his face.

12. I was f_____ to be tied.

13. That dress fl_____ her.

14. I have a spl_____ headache.

15. I am forever f_____ laundry.

16. I can't believe he was perm_____ to do that.

17. I hope you're not ups_____ with me.

18. Always be careful around a w_____ animal.

19. It's not funny when someone sh_____ you around.

20. I'm sorry I forg_____ to say, "I'm sorry."

	41st day	42nd day	43rd day	44th day
1.	**show**	shows	showed	showing
2.	**low**	lower	lowest	lowly
3.	**blow**	blows	blown	blowing
4.	blower	slower	slowest	slowly
5.	**slow**	slows	slowed	slowing
6.	flow	flows	flowed	flowing
7.	glow	glows	glowed	glowing
8.	below	grower	growers	a grownup
9.	**grow**	grows	* **grown**	growing
10.	outgrow	outgrows	outgrown	outgrowing
11.	crow	crows	crowed	crowing
12.	**stove**	stoves	drove	droves
13.	rove	roves	roved	roving
14.	grove	groves	trove	strove
15.	Jove	Jove's grove	wove	**was**
16.	cove	coves	** **does**	**does**
17.	he ** **dove** in	a white **dove**	white doves	**doesn't**
18.	clove	cloves	He **dove**	**wasn't**
19.	**over**	overs	overly	Passover
20.	clover	clovers	clover	clover
21.	rover	rovers	drover	drovers
22.	slower than	slowest	slowly	a good eye
23.	grower	growers	couldn't	would
24.	mow	mows	mowed	mowing
25.	mower	mowers	eyes	shouldn't

.
** **Heteronyms:**

does ("duz")	Does she or doesn't she fix breakfast?
does ("d'OH-z")	I saw one doe in the forest; John saw two does.
dove ("duv")	He painted a dove holding an olive branch.
dove ("d'OH-v")	She dove for cover. Her English teacher dived for cover.

* **Homophones:**

grown	I can't believe how fast that tree has grown.
groan	A bad joke makes me groan instead of laugh.

See the complete -ow family on pp. 310 & 684 in *The Patterns of English Spelling* (TPES); the -ove, p. 326; the -ver, p. 670.

	45th day	46th day	47th day	48th day
1.	robe	robes	robed	robing
2.	disrobe	disrobes	disrobed	disrobing
3.	probe	probes	probed	probing
4.	lobe	lobes	globe	**wasn't**
5.	globe	globes	global	**doesn't**
6.	code	codes	coded	coding
7.	decode	decodes	decoded	decoding
8.	explode	explodes	exploded	exploding
9.	* **rode**	rode	rode	rode
10.	erode	erodes	eroded	eroding
11.	* **road**	roads	a good road	doesn't
12.	railroad	railroads	railroaded	railroading
13.	* **toad**	toads	loader	loaders
14.	load	loads	loaded	loading
15.	reload	reloads	reloaded	reloading
16.	unload	unloads	unloaded	unloading
17.	overload	overloads	overloaded	overloading
18.	broad	abroad	broadly	abroad
19.	broaden	broadens	broadened	broadening
20.	**day**	* **days**	a * **day's** pay	two **days'** pay
21.	pay	pays	**paid**	paying
22.	repay	repays	repaid	repaying
23.	gay	gaily	gaily	broader than
24.	Fay	daily	daily	does
25.	shouldn't	couldn't	wouldn't	doesn't

* Homophones:

rode	She rode the horse while the prisoner walked.
road	Do you know what road she took out of town?
rowed	She rowed the boat gently down the stream.
toad	A toad looks like a frog painted brown.
towed	The tow truck towed our car to the garage.
toed	We all toed the line.
days	How many days until Saturday?
daze	That man seems to be in a daze.
day's	He lost a day's pay.
days'	She lost two days' pay.

The complete -ove family is found on p. 326 in *The Patterns of English Spelling* (TPES); the -over, p. 670; the -obe, p. 320, the -ode, p. 323; -oad, p. 403; the -ay, p. 301.

	49th day	50th day	51st day	52nd day
1.	**today**	today's pay	Sunday	Monday
2.	bay	bays	gay	hay
3.	jay	jays	ray	* **rays**
4.	lay	lays	laid	laying
5.	repay	repays	repaid	repaying
6.	delay	delays	delayed	delaying
7.	relay	relays	relayed	relaying
8.	**play**	plays	played	playing
9.	display	displays	displayed	displaying
10.	replay	replays	replayed	replaying
11.	**they**	they are	they are	they are
12a.	** **gray**	* **grays**	* **grayed**	**graying**
12b.	** **grey**	* **greys**	* **greyed**	**greying**
13.	* **pray**	* **prays**	* **prayed**	**praying**
14.	* **prey**	* **preys**	* **preyed**	**preying**
15.	prayer	prayers	**wasn't**	**doesn't**
16.	tray	trays	Fay	Fay's toys
17.	portray	portrays	portrayed	portraying
18.	**boy**	boys	a boy's toy	boys' toys
19.	**toy**	toys	toyed	toying
20.	joy	joys	Ray	Ray's trays
21	enjoy	enjoys	enjoyed	enjoying
22.	coy	coyly	Roy	Roy's
23.	Troy	ploy	Troy's ploys	enjoyment
24.	destroy	destroys	destroyed	destroying
25.	annoy	annoys	annoyed	annoying

* Homophones:

pray/prey	Do Eskimos pray for snow? Hawks prey on smaller birds
prays/preys/praise	A religious person prays quite often. The lion preys on smaller animals. Everybody needs a little praise now and then.
prayed/preyed	We prayed hoping the lion preyed on zebras not us.
grays/greys/graze	Some grays (greys) are darker than others. Some animals graze on grass.
grayed/greyed	The man's hair grayed (greyed) overnight.
grade	What grade do you expect to get in here?
rays/raise/raze	The sun's rays can burn the skin. Raise your hand if you have a question. To raze a building is to tear it down.

See the complete -ay family on p. 301 in *The Patterns of English Spelling* (TPES); the
    -ey, p. 302; the -oy, p. 303.

30

	53rd day	54th day	55th day	56th day
1.	slay	slays	slayer	slaying
2.	clay	**away**	always	Kay
3.	**say**	**says**	**said**	saying
4.	stray	strays	strayed	straying
5.	fray	*** frays**	frayed	fraying
6.	**may**	**always**	jay	jays
7.	**stay**	stays	stayed	staying
8.	oak	oaks	oaken	**wasn't**
9.	soak	soaks	soaked	soaking
10.	cloak	cloaks	cloaked	cloaking
11.	croak	croaks	croaked	croaking
12.	goal	goals	Joan	Joan's loan
13.	coal	coals	**does**	**doesn't**
14.	*** loan**	loans	loaned	loaning
15.	*** moan**	moans	moaned	moaning
16.	*** groan**	groans	groaned	groaning
17.	**own**	owns	owned	owning
18.	owner	owners	flown	**were**
19.	*** grown**	grownups	unknown	**weren't**
20.	*** thrown**	**known**	*** shown**	unknown
21.	flown	flown	unsaid	owner
22.	blown	blown up	blown down	shouldn't
23.	*** shown**	new **mown** hay	**thrown**	**thrown down**
24.	disown	disowns	disowned	disowning
25.	overgrown	homegrown	well known	brown eyes

* Homophones:

frays / phrase	A cheap shirt frays quickly at the collar. A phrase is just a group of words.
loan	Could you loan me some money until tomorrow?
lone	Who do you think I am, the Lone Ranger? (loan arranger?)
moan / mown	Bad puns make me moan and groan. I love the smell of new mown hay.
thrown	He was thrown out of the game for arguing with the umpire.
throne	When did Queen Elizabeth I first sit on the throne?
grown	Have you grown accustomed to my face?
groan	I just knew that would draw a groan from some of you.
shown	We were shown all around the center.
shone	The sun had shone brightly most of the day.

The complete -ay family is found on pp. 301 in TPES; the -ey, p. 302; the -oak, p. 409, the -oal, p. 413; -oan, p. 421; the -own, p. 421.

	57th day	58th day	59th day	60th day
1.	**car**	cars	**far**	afar
2.	bar	bars	* **barred**	barring
3.	jar	jars	jarred	jarring
4.	tar	tars	tarred	tarring
5.	**star**	stars	starred	starring
6.	arch	arches	arched	arching
7.	**march**	marches	marched	marching
8.	March	March's wind	**were**	**weren't**
9.	starch	starches	starched	starching
10.	archer	archers	archery	**doesn't**
11.	card	cards	carded	carding
12.	discard	discards	discarded	discarding
13.	regard	regards	regarded	regarding
14.	disregard	disregards	disregarded	disregarding
15.	yard	yards	lard	**wasn't**
16.	guard	guards	guarded	guarding
17.	unguard	unguards	unguarded	unguarding
18.	safeguard	safeguards	safeguarded	safeguarding
19.	hard	harder	hardest	hardly
20.	Miss Hardy	tardy	tardiness	hardiness
21.	dime	dimes	lime	limes
22.	* **time**	times	timed	timing
23.	crime	crimes	slime	**doesn't**
24.	rime	rimes	**doesn't**	**wouldn't**
25.	rhyme	rhymes	rhymed	rhyming

* Homophones:

time	What time is it?
thyme	Rosemary, sage, and thyme are all spices.
barred	The poet was barred from reciting his poems.
bard	The bard's poetry was censored;

What do you call a censored poet? Answer: A barred bard.

The complete -ar family is found on p. 501 in *The Patterns of English Spelling* (TPES); the -arch, p. 505;, the -ard, p. 505; the -ime, p. 333.

32

	61st day	62nd day	63rd day	64th day
1.	**home**	homes	homed	homing
2.	dome	domes	domed	doming
3.	* **Rome**	**Rome's** homes	**Nome**	Nome's homes
4.	**gnome**	**gnomes**	Homer	Homer's home
5.	foam	foams	foamed	foaming
6.	* **roam**	**roams**	roamed	roaming
7.	**soap**	soaps	soaped	soaping
8.	oat	oats	overcoat	overcoats
9.	**coat**	coats	coated	coating
10.	**boat**	boats	goat	goats
11.	float	floats	floated	floating
12.	bloat	bloats	bloated	bloating
13.	throat	throats	* **moat**	moats
14.	**and**	grand	overhand	underhand
15.	**stand**	stands	stood	standing
16.	understand	understands	understood	understanding
17.	misunderstand	misunderstands	misunderstood	misunderstanding
18.	slander	slanders	slandered	slandering
19.	Anderson	**wasn't**	**doesn't**	**weren't**
20.	chime	chimes	chimed	chiming
21.	prime	primes	primed	priming
22.	mime	mimes	mimed	miming
23.	floater	floaters	good eyes	shouldn't
24.	goat	goats	We would do it.	I'm going.
25.	boater	boaters	He does it.	He didn't do it.

* Homophones:

Rome	Rome wasn't built in a day.
roam	I would like to roam all over the world.
gnome	Have you ever seen a gnome?
Nome	Have you ever been in Nome?
moat	Never go swimming in a moat.
mote	A mote is a speck of dust.

What do you call a wandering Italian? Answer: A roamin' Roman.

What do you call Alaskan elves? Answer: Nome's gnomes.

The complete -ome family is found on p. 333 in TPES; the -ime, p. 333; the -oam, p. 418; -oap, 425; -oat, 429; -and, 227.

	65th day	66th day	67th day	68th day
1.	**end**	ends	ended	ending
2.	bend	* **bends**	bent	bending
3.	lend	* **lends**	lent	lending
4.	blend	blends	blended	blending
5.	depend	depends	depended	depending
6.	suspend	suspends	suspended	suspending
7.	**spend**	spends	spent	spending
8.	pipe	pipes	piped	piping
9.	windpipe	windpipes	bagpipe	bagpipes
10.	ripe	ripen	ripens	ripened
11.	gripe	gripes	griped	griping
12.	wipe	wipes	wiped	wiping
13.	swipe	swipes	swiped	swiping
14.	* **band**	* **bands**	banded	banding
15.	disband	disbands	disbanded	disbanding
16.	land	lands	landed	landing
17.	brand	brands	branded	branding
18.	time	times	timed	timing
19.	sometime	sometimes	bedtime	daytime
20.	overtime	grime	crime	crimes
21.	crime	crimes	criminal	criminals
22.	lime	limes	slime	grime
23.	timer	timers	timely	meantime
24.	friend	friends	friendly	friendlier
25.	befriend	befriends	befriended	befriending

* Homophones:

bends	A good staff bends without breaking.
Ben's	Ben's staff broke.
lends	An eye doctor lends a helping hand.
lens	I need a new lens for my camera.
band	The band was not allowed to play in the park.
banned	You might say the band was banned from playing in the park.
bands	There are many different types of bands.
bans	When a city bans bands, they won't have any music in their park.

The complete -end family is found on p. 228 in TPES; the -ipe, p. 341; the -and, p. 227; the -ime, p. 333.

	69th day	70th day	71st day	72nd day
1.	mend	* **mends**	mended	mending
2.	commend	commends	commended	commending
3.	recommend	recommends	recommended	recommending
4.	tend	tends	tended	tending
5.	pretend	pretends	pretended	pretending
6.	**send**	sends	sent	sending
7.	fend	fends	fended	fending
8.	offend	offends	offended	offending
9.	defend	defends	defended	defending
10.	tripe	wiper	wipers	doesn't
11.	stripe	stripes	striped	striping
12.	snipe	snipes	sniped	sniping
13.	sniper	snipers	**was**	**wasn't**
14.	**sand**	sands	sanded	sanding
15.	strand	strands	stranded	stranding
16.	demand	demands	demanded	demanding
17.	command	commands	commanded	commanding
18.	commander	commanders	commandment	commandments
19.	expand	expands	expanded	expanding
20.	bland	gland	glands	grander
21.	**does**	**doesn't**	**were**	**weren't**
22.	hand	hands	handed	handing
23.	underhand	handy	underhanded	handier
24.	homeland	beforehand	grandma	grandest
25.	shouldn't	wouldn't	grandpa	couldn't

* Homophones:

men's	They went into the men's clothing department looking for hats.
mends	A seamstress mends clothing.
	(Why don't we have seamsters or teamstresses?)

The complete -end family is found on p. 228 in TPES; the -ipe, p. 341; the -and, p. 227; the -ime, p. 333.

73rd day	74th day	75th day	76th day
1. intend	intends	intended	intending
2. attend	attends	attended	attending
3. extend	extends	extended	extending
4. amend	amends	amended	amending
5. vend	vends	vended	vending
6. **friend**	friends	friendly	friendlier
7. befriend	befriends	befriended	befriending
8. attend	attends	attended	attending
9. type	types	typed	typing
10. retype	retypes	retyped	retyping
11. * **bite**	bites	**bit**	biting
12. * **write**	writes	* **wrote**	**writing**
13. writer	writers	**written**	**written**
14. rewrite	rewrites	rewrote	rewriting
15. * **cite**	cites	cited	citing
16. recite	recites	recited	reciting
17. excite	excites	excited	exciting
18. **kite**	kites	* **mite**	mites
19. * **site**	sites	* **might**	mighty
20. * **sight**	sights	sighted	sighting
21. **light**	lights	lit	lighting
22. slight	slights	slighted	slighting
23. lighter	lightest	lightly	slightly
24. lender	lenders	spender	spenders
25. blender	blenders	suspender	suspenders

* Homophones:

bite	Who took a bite from my apple?
byte	Computers measure capacity by bytes, whatever they are.
right	Yes, that's right. It's all right. "Alright," already!
rite	A rite and a ritual are related. Both are ceremonies.
write	Everybody should know how to read and write.
Wright	The name Wright means to make. Think about Cartwright.
sight	Out of sight; out of mind.
cite	A judge can cite you for contempt.
site	Be careful walking around a construction site.
wrote	He wrote a long letter.
rote	He knew all his prayers by rote.
mite	You don't want to find a mite on your head.
might	You might not like to find a louse either.

The complete -end family is found on p. 228 in TPES; the -ipe (-ype), p. 341; the -ite, p. 357; the -ight, p. 428.

	77th day	78th day	79th day	80th day
1.	**white**	whites	**does**	**doesn't**
2.	polite	politely	politeness	impolite
3.	unite	unites	united	uniting
4.	reunite	reunites	reunited	reuniting
5.	union	unions	unity	United States
6.	reunion	reunions	unify	unified
7.	**quite** so	**quite** nice	**quite** good	**quite** a bite
8.	* **right**	rights	righted	righting
9.	**all right**	upright	downright	might
10.	fight	fights	fought	fighting
11.	fright	* **night**	nights	upright
12.	frighten	frightens	frightened	frightening
13.	tight	* **knight**	knights	bolts of **lightning**
14.	tighten	tightens	tightened	tightening
15.	lighten	lightens	lightened	lightening
16.	flight	flights	braver	bravery
17.	bright	brighter	brightest	* **Brighton**
18.	* **brighten**	brightens	brightened	brightening
19.	**save**	saves	saved	saving
20.	**safe**	safely	safety	safeties
21.	pave	paves	paved	paving
22.	shave	shaves	shaved	shaving
23.	rave	raves	raved	raving
24.	**brave**	braves	braved	braving
25.	fighter	fighters	**were**	**weren't**

* Homophones:

right	Yes, that's right. It's all right. "Alright," already!
rite	A rite and a ritual are related. Both are ceremonies.
write	Everybody should know how to read and write.
Wright	The name Wright means to make. Think about Cartwright.
brighten/Brighton	Street lights might brighten Brighton.
night	We had to work day and night.
knight	A knight sometimes wore a suit of armor.

The complete -end family is found on p. 228 in TPES; the -ipe (-ype), p. 341; the -ite, p. 357; the -ight, p. 428; -ave, p. 324.

Evaluation Test #2 (After 80 Days)

		Pattern being tested	Lesson word is in
1.	A bully is always sh**oving** others around.	oving	40
2.	I like to play "Sh**ow** and Tell." Don't you?	ow	41
3.	We dr**ove** there, but it took us four hours.	ove	43
4.	He's just bl**owing** off steam.	owing	44
5.	We got him a bath r**obe** for his birthday.	obe	45
6.	She really expl**oded**.	oded	47
7.	I really enj**oy** listening to good music.	oy	49
8.	The airplane was del**ayed** by fog.	ayed	51
9.	I l**oaned** Pat five dollars a week ago.	oaned	55
10.	We got s**oaking** wet.	oaking	56
11.	Cr**ime** doesn't pay.	ime	57
12.	They left the dump ungu**arded**.	arded	59
13.	Have you seen a movie st**arring** Bob Hope?	arring	60
14.	Do you like to watch soldiers m**arching**?	arching	60
15.	There's no place like h**ome**.	ome	61
16.	We need a new bar of s**oap**.	oap	61
17.	We came to an underst**anding**.	anding	64
18.	It all dep**ends** upon your point of view.	ends	66
19.	They dem**anded** equal rights.	anded	71
20.	The movie was very exc**iting**.	iting	76

Name_____ Date_____

Evaluation Test #2

1. A bully is always sh_____ others around.

2. I like to play "Sh_____ and Tell." Don't you?

3. We dr_____ there, but it took us four hours.

4. He's just bl_____ off steam.

5. We got him a bath r_____ for his birthday.

6. She really expl_____.

7. I really enj_____ listening to good music.

8. The airplane was del_____ by fog.

9. I l_____ Pat five dollars a week ago.

10. We got s_____ wet.

11. Cr_____ doesn't pay.

12. They left the dump ungu_____.

13. Have you seen a movie st_____ Bob Hope?

14. Do you like to watch soldiers m_____ ?

15. There's no place like h_____.

16. We need a new bar of s_____.

17. We came to an underst_____.

18. It all dep_____ upon your point of view.

19. They dem_____ equal rights.

20. The movie was very exc_____.

	81st day	82nd day	83rd day	84th day
1.	grave	graves	Dave	Dave's cave
2.	cave	caves	caved	caving
3.	**gave**	forgave	**does**	**doesn't**
4.	engrave	engraves	engraved	engraving
5.	engraver	slaver	slavery	bravery
6.	crave	craves	craved	craving
7.	slave	slaves	slaved	slaving
8.	enslave	enslaves	enslaved	enslaving
9.	* **wave**	waves	waved	waving
10.	behave	behaves	behaved	behaving
11.	misbehave	misbehaves	misbehaved	misbehaving
12.	**have**	has	**had**	having
13.	leaf	leafs	leafed	leafing
14.	leave	leaves	**left**	leaving
15.	oaf	oafs	**were**	**weren't**
16.	to loaf	loafs	loafed	loafing
17.	one loaf	two loaves	**was**	**wasn't**
18.	goof	goofs	goofed	goofing
19.	roof	roofs	roofed	roofing
20.	proof	proofs	foolproof	goofproof
21.	spoof	spoofs	spoofed	spoofing
22.	prove	proves	proved	proving
23.	approve	approves	approved	approving
24.	move	moves	moved	moving
25.	mover	movers	movie	movies

** **Heteronyms: have/have/have**

"hav" a transitive verb   I have a pencil.
"uv" an auxiliary verb   I should have known better.
"haf" half of verb phrase: *"Hafta" is correctly spelled have to* as in I *have to* go.

> You should **have** ("uv") known, we would **have to** ("haf tuh") **have** ("hav") an example of all three *haves* in one sentence.

* **Homophones:**

wave   Little children love to wave good-bye.
waive   Lawyers rarely waive their rights.
The complete -ave family is on p. 324 in TPES; the -eaf, p. 406; -oaf, p. 407; -oof, p. 407.

	85th day	86th day	87th day	88th day
1.	**lift**	lifts	lifted	lifting
2.	**gift**	gifts	gifted	swift
3.	sift	sifts	sifted	sifting
4.	swift	rift	rifts	thrift
5.	drift	drifts	drifted	drifting
6.	shift	shifts	shifted	shifting
7.	off	soft	softy	lofty
8.	doff	doffs	doffed	doffing
9.	scoff	scoffs	scoffed	scoffing
10.	oft'	**often**	often	often
11.	**soft**	softly	softer	softest
12.	soften	softens	softened	softening
13.	loft	lofts	lofted	lofting
14.	aloft	mall	malls	pitfall
15.	* **all**	**small**	smaller	smallest
16.	**tall**	taller	tallest	snowfall
17.	stall	stalls	stalled	stalling
18.	install	installs	installed	installing
19.	installment	installments	**fall**	falls
20.	**call**	calls	called	calling
21.	recall	recalls	recalled	recalling
22.	**wall**	walls	walled	walling
23.	**ball**	balls	football	footballs
24.	**were**	**weren't**	**isn't**	**doesn't**
25.	**does**	**doesn't**	**wasn't**	**shouldn't**

* Homophones:

| all | I can't believe I ate all that pie. |
| awl | A carpenter should know how to use an awl. |

The complete -ift family is found on p. 232 in TPES; the-oft, p. 232; -all, 147.

Parent/Teacher Note: The word doff is the opposite of don. Doff means to take off. Don means to put on as in "Don we now our gay apparel," which means "Let's put on our best clothes." Men used to doff their hats when meeting a lady.

	89th day	90th day	91st day	92nd day
1.	ill	ills	**does**	**doesn't**
2.	*** fill**	fills	filled	filling
3.	refill	refills	refilled	refilling
4.	fulfill	fulfills	fulfilled	fulfilling
5.	filler	fillers	**were**	**weren't**
6.	filch	filches	filched	filching
7.	pill	pills	**was**	**wasn't**
8.	spill	spills	spilled	spilling
9.	till	tills	**until**	**until**
10.	still	stills	stilled	stilling
11.	half	halves	half	halves
12.	calf	calves	calf	a calf's tail
13.	elf	elves	yourself	**were**
14.	self	selves	**myself**	ourselves
15.	himself	herself	itself	**weren't**
16.	shelf	shelves	fig	figs
17.	**big**	bigger	biggest	jig
18.	**dig**	digs	dug	digging
19.	**pig**	pigs	digger	diggers
20.	rig	*** rigs**	rigged	rigging
21.	wig	wigs	twig	twigs
22.	swig	swigs	swigged	swigging
23.	wiggle	wiggles	wiggled	wiggling
24.	giggle	giggles	giggled	giggling
25.	trigger	triggers	triggered	triggering

* Homophones:

fill	Fill it up, please.
Phil	Phil's full name is either Phillip or Phyllis.
rigs	That shop rigs out and rents all kinds of fishing equipment.
Riggs	Mr. and Mrs. Riggs were both invited.
jigs/Jiggs	Both Jiggs and Maggie love to dance jigs.

See the complete -ill family on p. 151 in *The Patterns of English Spelling* (TPES); the -alf, p. 243; the -elf, p. 243; the -ig, p. 113.

	93rd day	94th day	95th day	96th day
1.	Bill	Bill's pills	**won't**	**won't**
2.	bill	bills	*** billed**	billing
3.	gill	gills	*** build**	**building**
4.	kill	kills	killed	killing
5.	skill	skills	skilled	unskilled
6.	mill	mills	milled	milling
7.	**will**	wills	willed	willing
8.	chill	chills	chilled	chilling
9.	rill	rills	dill	dills
10.	trill	trills	trilled	trilling
11.	thrill	thrills	thrilled	thrilling
12.	**dog**	dogs	frog	frogs
13.	jog	jogs	jogged	jogging
14.	jogger	joggers	goggles	toggle
15.	hog	hogs	hogged	hogging
16.	log	logs	logged	logging
17.	flog	flogs	flogged	flogging
18.	smog	grog	groggy	**doesn't**
19.	cog	cogs	tog	togs
20.	clog	clogs	clogged	clogging
21.	**wasn't**	**weren't**	**didn't**	**don't**
22.	elf	elves	**chilly**	**silliest**
23.	shelf	shelves	shelved	shelving
24.	**half**	halves	**chili**	**sillier**
25.	calf	calves	**silly**	Billy

* Homophones:

billed   I hate to be billed for something I didn't buy.
build   They are going to build tractors in the old tank factory.
chili / chilly   I like my chili hot not chilly.
The complete -ill family is found on p. 151 in TPES; the -og, p. 114.

	97th day	98th day	99th day	100th day
1.	drill	drills	drilled	drilling
2.	grill	grills	grilled	grilling
3.	**girl**	**girls**	**girl**	**girls**
4.	frill	frills	shrill	dill
5.	**hill**	hills	uphill	downhill
6.	eel	eels	**does**	**doesn't**
7.	**feel**	feels	felt	**feeling**
8.	* **heel**	heels	heeled	heeling
9.	* **peel**	peels	peeled	peeling
10.	wheel	wheels	* **steel**	steel
11.	* **real**	**really**	unreal	**really**
12.	* **heal**	heals	healed	healing
13.	seal	seals	sealed	sealing
14.	* **steal**	steals	stole	stealing
15.	**meal**	**meals**	**wasn't**	**weren't**
16.	veal	zeal	**can't**	**didn't**
17.	reveal	reveals	revealed	revealing
18.	deal	deals	** **dealt**	dealing
19.	* **peal**	peals	pealed	pealing
20.	appeal	appeals	appealed	appealing
21.	* **cereal**	cereals	series	serious
22.	* **serial**	serials	serial	cereal
23.	hilly	sealer	sealers	The Steelers
24.	dealer	dealers	peeler	peelers
25.	healer	healers	**isn't**	**wasn't**

* Homophones:

heel	Have you taught your dog how to heel?
heal	A sprained ankle just takes time to heal.
peel	Bananas are easier to peel than apples, oranges, and grapes.
peal	Did you hear that peal of thunder?
reel	Fishermen just love to reel in fish.
real	What is the real thing?
steel	Superman is the man of steel.
steal	Everybody knows it's wrong to steal.
cereal	Many people eat cereal for breakfast.
serial	American soldiers are given serial numbers.

**   dealt is pronounced "delt"! Cf. feel/felt.
The complete -ill family is found on p. 151 in TPES; the -eel, p. 412; the -eal, p. 412.

	101st day	102nd day	103rd day	104th day
1.	**book**	**books**	booked	booking
2.	**cook**	**cooks**	**cooked**	**cooking**
3.	cookbook	cookbooks	cookie	cookies
4.	rook	rooks	**We were there.**	**They weren't here.**
5.	crook	crooks	crooked	won't
6.	brook	brooks	shook	don't
7.	hook	hooks	hooked	hooking
8.	unhook	unhooks	unhooked	unhooking
9.	**look**	**looks**	**looked**	**looking**
10.	overlook	overlooks	overlooked	overlooking
11.	outlook	outlook	took	nook
12.	squeal	squeals	squealed	squealing
13.	repeal	repeals	repealed	repealing
14.	conceal	conceals	concealed	concealing
15.	**take**	takes	**taken**	**taking**
16.	** **sake**	sakes	**can't**	**doesn't**
17.	shake	shakes	**wasn't**	shaking
18.	fake	fakes	faked	faking
19.	**bake**	bakes	baked	baking
20.	**cake**	cakes	caked	caking
21.	baker	bakers	bakery	bakeries
22.	**ache**	**aches**	**ached**	**aching**
23.	18 wheeler	18 wheelers	**shouldn't**	**wouldn't**
24.	feeler	feelers	feeling	shakers
25.	squealer	squealers	Man of Steel	stealing

** **Heteronyms:**
sake ("SAY'k")   Please do it for my sake.
sake ("SAH kay")   The Japanese make a wine called sake out of rice.

**   The "k" sound in words that came into our language from the Greek are usually spelled with a "ch." These words usually are either religious words such as **Ch**rist (**K**-ryh'st) or medical terms such as a**ch**e and **ch**ronic. See pp. 905-908 in *The Patterns of English Spelling* for complete listing of words in which the "k" sound is spelled ch.

See the complete-ook family is found on p. 409 in TPES; the -eal, p. 412; -ake, p. 328 in *The Patterns of English Spelling* (TPES).

	105th day	106th day	107th day	108th day
1.	lake	lakes	wasn't	weren't
2.	flake	flakes	flaked	flaking
3.	make	makes	* made	making
4.	rake	rakes	raked	raking
5.	* brake	brakes	braked	braking
6.	* break	breaks	broke	breaking
7.	breaker	breakers	breakage	unbreakable
8.	* steak	steaks	broken	breakfast
9.	* stake	stakes	staked	staking
10.	wake	wakes	woke	waking
11.	snake	snakes	snaked	snaking
12.	quake	quakes	quaked	quaking
13.	drake	drakes	can't	doesn't
14.	** ache	aches	ached	aching
15.	headache	headaches	backache	backaches
16.	toothache	toothaches	won't	don't
17.	bike	bikes	dike	dikes
18.	biker	bikers	Quaker	Quakers
19.	like	likes	liked	liking
20.	dislike	dislikes	disliked	disliking
21.	pike	pikes	should	shouldn't
22.	spike	spikes	spiked	spiking
23.	alike	look-alike	dike	unlike
24.	trike	trikes	Mike	unlikely
25.	strike	strikes	strikers	striking

* Homophones:

made	Tom made up his bed before he went to breakfast.
maid	Mary thought it would be nice if she had her own maid do it.
brake	We brake for animals.
break	Be careful. You might break something.
stake	We stake up our tomato plants.
steak	Once a year I have a juicy T-bone steak.

** The "k" sound in words that came into our language from the Greek are usually spelled with a "ch." These words usually are either religious words such as **Ch**rist (**K**-ryh'st) or medical terms such as a**ch**e and **ch**ronic. See pp. 905-908 in *The Patterns of English Spelling* for complete listing of words in which the "k" sound is spelled ch.

See the complete -ake family on p. 328 in *The Patterns of English Spelling* (TPES). the -eak, p. 408; the -ache, p. 906; the ike, p. 329.

46

	109th day	110th day	111th day	112th day
1.	hike	hikes	hiked	hiking
2.	hiker	hikers	* would	wouldn't
3.	mike	mikes	should	shouldn't
4.	Mike	Mike's bikes	could	couldn't
5.	trike	trikes	didn't	can't
6.	strike	strikes	struck	striking
7.	striker	strikers	token	tokens
8.	coke	cokes	broke	broken
9.	spoke	spokes	spoken	Hoboken
10.	weren't	isn't	won't	don't
11.	joke	jokes	joked	joking
12.	joker	jokers	poker	pokers
13.	choke	chokes	choked	choking
14.	poke	pokes	poked	poking
15.	smoke	smokes	smoked	smoking
16.	smoker	smokers	isn't	wasn't
17.	stroke	strokes	stroked	stroking
18.	* yoke	yokes	wool	wool
19.	* yolk	yolks	woolen	woolen
20.	folk	folks	woolly	woolly
21.	rule	rules	ruled	ruling
22.	ruler	rulers	yule	weren't
23.	overrule	overrules	overruled	overruling
24.	mule	mules	Jules	Julie
25.**	schedule	schedules	scheduled	scheduling

* Homophones:

yoke	Do you know what a yoke of oxen is?
yolk	An egg yolk is very high in cholesterol.
wood	Charlie McCarthy is a dummy made out of wood.
would	Would you like to have a dummy like Charlie McCarthy?
** Heteronyms:	Schedule is pronounced "SHED jul" in British English, "SKED jul in American English.

The complete -ike family is found on p. 329 in TPES; the -oke, p. 329; -olk, p. 245; -ule, 331.

	113th day	114th day	115th day	116th day
1.	**ear**	**ears**	earring	earrings
2.	**near**	nears	neared	nearing
3.	* **dear**	dears	dearest	**hasn't**
4.	**fear**	fears	feared	fearing
5.	* **hear**	**hears**	* **heard**	**hearing**
6.	overhear	overhears	overheard	overhearing
7.	gear	gears	geared	gearing
8.	**rear**	rears	reared	rearing
9.	beard	beards	bearded	bearding
10.	clear	clearly	Lake Erie	eerie
11.	* **deer**	queer	**deer**	queer
12.	* **beer**	beers	**haven't**	**didn't**
13.	**cheer**	cheers	cheered	cheering
14.	steer	steers	steered	steering
15.	sneer	sneers	sneered	sneering
16.	* **peer**	peers	peered	peering
17.	**ace**	aces	aced	acing
18.	**face**	faces	faced	facing
19.	pace	paces	* **paced**	pacing
20.	lace	laces	laced	lacing
21.	**place**	places	placed	placing
22.	replace	replaces	replaced	replacing
23.	shoelace	shoelaces	shoelace	shoelaces
24.	deface	defaces	defaced	defacing
25.	anyplace	paleface	someplace	**shouldn't**

* Homophones:

dear	Dear John, Dear Mary, Dear Mom, Dear Dad, ...
deer	I like to go to the zoo and watch the deer.
hear	You hear with your ear. Ear is in hear.
here	Come here or go there. Here is in there.
heard	I heard you. You don't have to yell. I can hear even with one ear.
herd	Never be afraid of being run over by a herd of angry caterpillars.
beer	Some of my friends drink non-alcoholic beer.
bier	A bier is a stand to hold a coffin or display a corpse.
peer	A peer is a person of equal status in the community.
pier	Sometimes you can go fishing off a pier.
paced	He was so nervous he paced back and forth.
paste	You can make paste out of flour and water.
Erie / eerie	The UFO Club spotted an eerie light over Lake Erie.

See the complete -ear family on p. 531 in *The Patterns of English Spelling* (TPES); the -eer, p. 531; -ace, p. 343.

48

	117th day	118th day	119th day	120th day
1.	* **shear**	shears	sheared	shearing
2.	smear	smears	smeared	smearing
3.	spear	spears	speared	spearing
4.	**clear**	clears	cleared	clearing
5.	clearly	clearer	clearest	dearest
6.	**appear**	appears	appeared	appearing
7.	disappear	disappears	disappeared	disappearing
8.	** **tear**	** **tears**	tearful	tearfully
9.	**year**	**years**	**does**	**doesn't**
10.	* **deer**	reindeer	**deer**	reindeer
11.	* **sheer**	cheerful	* **sheer**	**haven't**
12.	cheerful	cheerfully	career	careers
13.	jeer	jeers	jeered	jeering
14.	queer	queerly	queerest	queerer
15.	pioneer	pioneers	pioneered	pioneering
16.	volunteer	volunteers	volunteered	volunteering
17.	misplace	misplaces	misplaced	misplacing
18.	displace	displaces	displaced	displacing
19.	fireplace	fireplaces	racer	racers
20.	**race**	races	raced	**racing**
21.	brace	braces	braced	bracing
22.	embrace	embraces	embraced	embracing
23.	trace	traces	traced	tracing
24.	Dick Tracy	lacy	Mr. Gacy	Mrs. Macy
25.	**weren't**	**wasn't**	**isn't**	**couldn't**

** **Heteronyms:**
tear ("TEER")   I hate to see anyone shed a tear.
tear ("TAY'r")   I hate to see anyone tear their clothes.

* **Homophones:**
tear ("TEER")   Tear drops went running down his cheek.
tier ("TEER")   We sat in the third row of the second tier of seats.

shear   Do you know how to shear a sheep?
sheer   Some costumes are made out of very sheer material.

dear/deer   What is a very special hart? A dear deer.
dear heart/deer heart   My dear heart wouldn't think of eating a deer heart or a hart
hart/heart   heart. (A hart is male deer, a buck)

The complete -ear family is found on p. 531 in TPES; the -eer, p. 531; the
       -ace, p. 343.

Evaluation Test #3 (After 120 Days)

	Pattern being tested	Lesson word is in
1. Those kids are always f**ighting**.	ighting	80
2. That means they're always misbeh**aving**.	aving	84
3. It's time for them to turn over a new l**eaf**.	eaf	81
4. I thought it was time to rake the l**eaves**.	eaves	82
5. It's time we sh**ifted** into high gear.	ifted	87
6. We're going to be inst**alling** a new system.	alling	88
7. My sister likes to f**ill** up our gas tank.	ill	89
8. I liked math about h**alf** the time.	alf	91
9. We keep our medicine on the highest sh**elf**.	elf	89
10. It was the b**iggest** jug I've ever seen.	iggest	91
11. They dr**illed** a new well last week.	illed	99
12. How are you f**eeling** today?	eeling	100
13. Too many c**ooks** spoil the broth.	ooks	102
14. They are always squ**ealing** their tires.	ealing	104
15. They were sh**aking** in their boots.	aking	104
16. We h**iked** all the way into town.	iked	111
17. Sm**oking** is not allowed in most public places.	oking	112
18. Everybody has r**ules** that they are to follow.	ules	110
19. My brother is very hard of h**earing**.	earing	116
20. Do we have any volunt**eers**?	eers	118

Name_____   Date_____

Evaluation Test #3

1. Their kids are always f_____.

2. That means they're always misbeh_____.

3. It's time for them to turn over a new l_____ .

4. I thought it was time to rake the l_____ .

5. It's time we sh_____ into high gear.

6. We're going to be inst_____ a new system.

7. My sister likes to f_____ up our gas tank.

8. I liked math about h_____ the time.

9. We keep our medicine on the highest sh_____.

10. It was the b_____ jug I've ever seen.

11. They dr_____ a new well last week.

12. How are you f_____ today?

13. Too many c_____ spoil the broth.

14. They are always squ_____ their tires.

15. They were sh_____ in their boots.

16. We h_____ all the way into town.

17. Sm_____ is not allowed in most public places.

18. Everybody has r_____ that they are to follow.

19. My brother is very hard of h_____ .

20. Do we have any volunt_____ ?

	121st day	122nd day	123rd day	124th day
1.	retrace	retraces	retraced	retracing
2.	grace	graces	graced	gracing
3.	**space**	spaces	spaced	spacing
4.	**ice**	ices	iced	icing
5.	**rice**	rices	riced	ricing
6.	**price**	prices	priced	pricing
7.	* **dice**	twice	thrice	lice
8.	vice	vices	advice	hasn't
9.	device	devices	Mr. Price	Mrs. Price
10.	lice	nice	mice	Ms. Price
11.	slice	slices	sliced	slicing
12.	splice	splices	spliced	splicing
13.	spice	spices	spiced	spicing
14.	**bang**	bangs	banged	banging
15.	**gang**	**gangs**	ganged	ganging
16.	clang	clangs	clanged	clanging
17.	fang	fangs	pang	pangs
18.	**sang**	**rang**	** brang	** swang
19.	**hang**	tang	slang	sprang
20.	hanger	hangers	**haven't**	**shouldn't**
21.	God	God's word	a god	many gods
22.	rod	rods	Roddy	trod
23.	nod	nods	nodded	nodding
24.	plod	plods	plodded	plodding
25.	prod	prods	prodded	prodding

* **dice** The word dice is plural. The singular is *die*! "The *die* is cast" means that only one *die* was thrown rather than two or more dice. Tool and die makers might argue the meaning of the phrase, the die is cast.

** **NOTE:** The words brang and swang are non-standard English and should not be used in any formal writing. Sometimes writers will use these spellings to indicate to the reader that the person using these words is uneducated.

See the complete -ace family on p. 343 in *The Patterns of English Spelling* (TPES); the -ice, p. 344; -ang, p. 217; -od, p. 109.

	125th day	126th day	127th day	128th day
1.	**bug**	**bugs**	bugged	bugging
2.	**rug**	**rugs**	** **rugged**	dug
3.	**drug**	**drugs**	drugged	drugging
4.	shrug	shrugs	shrugged	shrugging
5.	**hug**	hugs	hugged	hugging
6.	lug	lugs	lugged	lugging
7.	slug	slugs	slugged	slugging
8.	plug	plugs	plugged	plugging
9.	smuggle	smuggles	smuggling	smuggler
10.	snuggle	snuggles	snuggled	snuggling
11.	struggle	struggles	struggled	struggling
12.	range	ranges	ranged	ranging
13.	ranger	rangers	arranged	arranging
14.	**strange**	**stranger**	strangest	strangely
15.	**stranger**	**strangers**	**haven't**	**hasn't**
16.	arrange	arranges	**wasn't**	**weren't**
17.	arrangement	arrangements	**couldn't**	**wouldn't**
18.	rearrange	rearranges	rearranged	rearranging
19.	**change**	changes	changed	changing
20.	exchange	exchanges	exchanged	exchanging
21.	interchange	interchanges	interchanged	interchanging
22.	Red Grange	Miss Granger	danger	dangers
23.	**put**	**puts**	**put**	**putting**
24.	input	inputs	input	inputting
25.	output	**didn't**	**can't**	**don't**

** **Note:** The word *rugged* ("RUG gid")has two syllables. It is not related to the word *rug*.

Red Grange was a famous football player known as the "Galloping Ghost."
The complete -ug family is found on p. 115 in *The Patterns of English Spelling* (TPES); -ange, p. 367; -put, 135; -uggle, p 602.

	129th day	130th day	131st day	132nd day
1.	mug	mugs	mugged	mugging
2.	mugger	muggers	smug	snug
3.	slugger	sluggers	sluggish	snugly
4.	chug	chugs	chugged	chugging
5.	tug	tugs	tugged	tugging
6.	thug	thugs	jug	jugs
7.	* **but**	buts	nut	nuts
8.	* **butt**	butts	butted	butting
9.	**cut**	cuts	**haven't**	cutting
10.	rut	ruts	mutt	mutts
11.	gut	guts	gutted	gutting
12.	hut	huts	**doesn't**	**didn't**
13.	jut	juts	jutted	jutting
14.	strut	struts	strutted	strutting
15.	**shut**	shuts	**won't**	shutting
16.	nut	nuts	nutty	putty
17.	putt	putts	putted	** **putting**
18.	shuttle	shuttles	shuttled	shuttling
19.	button	buttons	buttoned	buttoning
20.	unbutton	unbuttons	unbuttoned	unbuttoning
21.	**kid**	**kids**	**kidded**	**kidding**
22.	skid	skids	skidded	skidding
23.	bid	bids	bid	bidding
24.	forbid	forbids	forbidden	forbidding
25.	stupid	stupidly	Mr. Stupid	stupid

** **Heteronyms:**

putting ("PuuT ing")   Are you putting me on?
putting ("PUT ing")   Good golfers have to practice their putting, even Tiger Woods.

* **Homophones:**

but   Please don't say, "Yeah, but..."
butt   It's not polite to butt in.

See the complete -ug family on p. 115 in *The Patterns of English Spelling* (TPES); the -ut, p. 135; -id, p. 108.

	133rd day	134th day	135th day	136th day
1.	* **hide**	hides	**hid**/hidden	**hiding**
2.	**slide**	slides	slid	sliding
3.	slider	sliders	**would**	**wouldn't**
4.	**ride**	**rides**	**rode**/ridden	**riding**
5.	**rider**	**riders**	**should**	**shouldn't**
	spider	spiders	Mr. Hyde	**didn't**
6.	bride	brides	the bride's ring	proud
7.	* **pride**	prides	prided	priding
8.	stride	strides	strode	striding
9.	**put**	**puts**	**put**	** **putting**
10.	input	inputs	input	inputting
11.	**did**	**didn't**	Sid	Sid's bid
12.	splendid	splendidly	lid	lids
13.	rid	rids	rid	ridding
14.	grid	grids	quid	squid
15.	lid	lids	valid	* **invalid**
16.	boo	boos	booed	booing
17.	bamboo	peekaboo	bugaboo	* **it's** * **too bad**
18.	booboo	booboos	boobooed	boobooing
19.	coo	coos	cooed	cooing
20.	moo	moos	mooed	mooing
21.	riddle	riddles	riddled	kiddy car
22.	griddle	griddles	hidden	fiddler
23.	fiddle	fiddles	fiddled	fiddling
24.	middle	middle	**stupid**	**Where** is it?
25.	**stupid**	boohoo	boohoos	boohooed

* Homophones:

hide	Where did you hide my pencil?
hied	To hie is to hurry someplace. He hied himself to work. This usage is archaic.
pride/pried	You should take pride in your work. The repairman pried open the stuck door.
two / to / too	One, two, three. Twin, twice, two. I want to... I have to... Too means so as in Too much, too fast, too hot, too cold, means also as in: We went there, and they did, too.
its / it's	Possessive. The dog hurt its (her/his) paw. Contraction: *It's* too bad means *it is* too bad.

Heteronyms:

putting ("PuuT ing")   You should be putting away your work.
putting ("PUT ing")   I need to practice my putting with my new putter.
invalid ("IN vuh lid" or "in VAL id") When I was an invalid, I called myself invalid.
The -ide family is found on p. 322 in TPES; the -put, 135; the -id, p. 108, -oo, p. 312.

55

	137th day	138th day	139th day	140th day
1.	decide	decides	decided	deciding
2.	decisive	decisively	decidedly	decision
3.	* **side**	sides	sided	siding
4.	**beside**	besides	inside	insides
5.	**outside**	bedside	wayside	backside
6.	divide	divides	dividing	division
7.	provide	provides	providing	provision
8.	collide	collides	collided	collision
9.	**wide**	snide	It's too hot.	It's too cold.
10.	widen	widens	widened	widening
11.	boohoo	boohoos	boohooed	boohooing
12.	voodoo	goo	blue goo	shmoo
13.	pooh	gooey	goo goose	weren't
14.	shampoo	shampoos	shampooed	shampooing
15.	**zoo**	zoos	Kalamazoo	Kalamazoo's zoo
16.	kangaroo	kangaroos	igloo	igloos
17.	* **shoo**	* **shoos**	shooed	shooing
18.	* **shoe**	* **shoes**	shoed	shoeing
19.	tattoo	tattoos	tattooed	tattooing
20.	taboo	taboos	* **would**	**wouldn't**
21.	tabu	shoeshine	shoebox	soft-shoe
22.	canoe	canoes	canoed	canoeing
23.	horseshoe	shoelaces	snowshoe	snowshoes
24.	Yahoo	peek-a-boo	bamboo	Waterloo
25.	water	waters	watered	watering

* Homophones:

side / sighed	Whose side are you on? She sighed a great big sigh.
shoe / shoo	The shoe is on the other foot now. Shoo fly don't bother me.
wood	The box was made out of wood, pine I think.
would	Would you please follow directions?

See the complete -ide family on p. 322 in *The Patterns of English Spelling* (TPES); the -oo, p. 312.

56

	141st day	142nd day	143rd day	144th day
1.	reside	resides	resided	residing
2.	resident	* **residents**	residential	**doesn't**
3.	preside	presides	presided	presiding
4.	president	presidents	presidential	**wasn't**
5.	confide	confides	confided	confiding
6.	confident	confidently	confidential	confidentially
7.	bide	bides	bided	biding
8.	* **tide**	tides	tided	tiding
9.	chide	chides	chided	chiding
10.	guide	guides	guided	guiding
11.	* **no**	I said no	**ago**	**also**
12.	**go**	**goes**	**went/gone**	**going**
13.	veto	vetoes	vetoed	vetoing
14.	**zero**	zeroes	zeroed	zeroing
15.	**hero**	heroes	zero	zeros
16.	* **solo**	solos	soloed	soloing
17.	piano	pianos	banjo	banjos
18.	trio	trios	radio	radios
19.	lasso	lassos	lassoed	lassoing
20.	patio	patios	ditto	dittos
21.	echo	echoes	echoed	echoing
22.	ditto	hello	potato	potatoes
23.	lasso	lassoes	lassoed	lassoing
24.	buffalo	buffaloes	tomato	tomatoes
25.	domino	dominoes	Negro	Negroes

* Homophones:

| residents | Not all of the residents in the project voted for her. |
| residence | She did not maintain her residence in that district. |

| tide | The ship left at high tide. |
| tied | The children all tied their own shoelaces. |

| no | No, you can't go. |
| know | You know what I mean. |

| solo | She sang a solo. |
| so low | Too bad she didn't sing so low we couldn't hear her. |

The complete -ide family is found on p. 322 in TPES; the -oo, p. 312, -ent, p. 250, -o ("OH"), p. 309.

	145th day	146th day	147th day	148th day
1.	* do	** does	doesn't	doing
2.	undo	undoes	undid	undoing
3.	to go	want to	have to	going to
4.	unto	into	onto	too much
5.	who	Who's coming?	Whose book is it?	two toys
6.	* toe	* toes	* toed	* toeing
7.	Joe	Joe's toes	foe	foes
8.	Joseph	Joseph's woes	Who's Moe?	Whose cat is that?
9.	woe	woes	Poe	Poe's a poet
10.	* doe	* does	tiptoe	tiptoes
11.	hoe	* hoes	hoed	hoeing
12.	low	lower	lowest	lowly
13.	blow	blows	blew/blown	blowing
14.	blower	blowers	grower	growers
15.	grow	grows	grew/grown	growing
16.	slow	slows	slowed	slowing
17.	flow	flows	flowed	flowing
18.	overflow	overflows	overflowed	overflowing
19.	* tow	* tows	* towed	* towing
20.	glow	glows	glowed	glowing
21.	mellow	mellows	mellowed	mellowing
22.	yellow	yellows	yellowed	yellowing
23.	bellow	bellows	bellowed	bellowing
24.	* know	* knows	Who * knew?	knowing
25.	No, I don't know.	The nose knows.	Whose * new car?	Who knows?

* Homophones:

do / due / dew	Do you know your book is due. Do you like to see the early morning dew.
tow/toe	My sister drove her toy tow truck over my big toe.
toed / toad /towed	We all toed the line or we were called a toad Our car had to be towed.
hoes / hose	My aunt hoes her garden every morning. My uncle bought her a new garden hose.
dough / doe	Bakeries make a lot of dough. Doe, a deer, a female deer.
allowed/aloud	We were not allowed to talk aloud in the library.
know / no /knows / nose	I know that no one knows exactly how the nose smells.
knew / new / gnu	I just knew you would talk about a zoo getting a new gnu.

Heteronyms:

does ("DOH'z" & DUZ)	Does are deer, female deer. Does that make any sense to you?

See the complete -o family on p. 312 in *The Patterns of English Spelling* (TPES);
the -oe, 311; the -ow ("OH"), p. 310.

	149th day	150th day	151st day	152nd day
1.	ow	ow	now	how
2.	wow	wows	wowed	wowing
3.	**cow**	**cows**	pow	powwow
4.	**how**	**somehow**	**anyhow**	pow
5.	vow	vows	vowed	vowing
6.	** bow	bows	bowed	**bowing**
7.	* plow	plows	plowed	plowing
8.	allow	allows	* allowed	allowing
9.	disallow	disallows	disallowed	disallowing
10.	brow	* brows	eyebrow	eyebrows
11.	a hay mow	hay mows	** sow	** sows
12.	hollow	hollows	hollowed	hollowing
13.	**follow**	**follows**	**followed**	**following**
14.	follower	followers	shallow	shallows
15.	wallow	wallows	wallowed	wallowing
16.	swallow	swallows	swallowed	swallowing
17.	**grow**	**grows**	**grew/grown**	**growing**
18.	grower	growers	can't	don't
19.	crow	crows	crowed	crowing
20.	**throw**	throws	* threw/* thrown	throwing
21.	* know	* knows	* knew/known	**knowing**
22.	**snow**	**snows**	**snowed**	**snowing**
23.	shadow	shadows	shadowed	shadowing
24	Who are you?	How do you do?	How are you?	Who is that?
25.	How can you?	Who did it?	Who am I?	How are you?

* Homophones:

bow	Let's bow our heads and pray.
bough	When the bough breaks, burn the branch.
plow	Farmers plow their fields in the spring.
plough	Farmers plough their fields in the fall.
brows	Farmers earn their living by the sweat of their brows.
browse	Let's go to a bookstore and browse around.
so / sew / sow	So what? Sew buttons or sow seeds.
no / know	No, you can't go. You know you can't go.
knows/nose	He thinks his nose knows everything.

**   Heteronyms:

bow ("B'OW!")	Bow your head.
bow ("B'OH")	Bow and arrow.
sow ("S'OW!")	A female pig is a sow. Rhymes with cow.
sow ("S'OH!)	You should sow your seeds early in the spring.

See the complete -ow ("OW") family p. 318 in TPES; the -ow ("OH"), p. 310.

	153rd day	154th day	155th day	156th day
1.	* **ease**	eases	eased	easing
2.	**easy**	**easier**	**easiest**	**easy**
3.	* **please**	pleases	pleased	pleasing
4.	**disease**	diseases	diseased	**pleasure**
5.	displease	displeases	displeased	displeasure
6.	**bad**	**badly**	**mad**	**madly**
7.	**a want * ad**	want ads	madder	maddest
8.	**sad**	sadly	sadder	saddest
9.	lad	lads	ladder	ladders
10.	**glad**	gladly	gladness	clad
11.	Ed	Ed's dad	**doesn't**	**weren't**
12.	wed	weds	wedded	**wedding**
13.	**bed**	beds	* **red**	bedding
14.	Fred	Fred's sled	Ned's sleds	bled
15.	**shed**	sheds	* **bred**	well-bred
16.	shred	shreds	shredded	shredding
17.	**bled**	pled	fled	sped
18.	* **pedal**	pedals	**flower petal**	petals
19.	* **medal**	medals	**metal**	metals
20.	* **peddle**	peddles	peddled	peddling
21.	* **meddle**	meddles	meddled	meddling
22.	* **size**	**sizes**	sized	sizing
23.	capsize	capsizes	capsized	capsizing
24.	baptize	baptizes	baptized	baptizing
25.	prize	prizes	prize	prizes

* Homophones:

E's / ease	It's not funny to get E's on tests. I hope this puts you at ease.
please / pleas	Please pay attention to our pleas.
ad / add	He bought a want ad. Everyone should know how to add.
red / read	Tom has red hair. Tom read a book about the red planet.
bred / bread	They bred a new breed of Siamese cats. I love good bread.
sighs / size	She sighs every time she thinks about her dress size.
meddle / medal	Don't meddle with a gold medal. Never peddle a broken pedal.
peddle / pedal	Don't try to peddle a broken pedal to me.

See the complete -ease family on p. 435 in *The Patterns of English Spelling* (TPES), the -ad, p. 106; -ed, p. 107, -ize p. 361.

60

	157th day	158th day	159th day	160th day
1.	* tease	teases	teased	teasing
2.	appease	appeases	appeased	appeasing
3.	please	pleasing	pleased	pleasingly
4.	pleasant	pleasures	pleasantly	unpleasant
5.	these	those	this	these
6.	wise	wisely	wiser than	wisest
7.	rise	rises	rose/risen	rising
8.	arise	arises	arose/arisen	arising
9.	sunrise	sunrises	pleasure	uprising
10.	surprise	surprises	surprised	surprising
11.	choose	chooses	chose	choosing
12.	lose	loses	Whose team won?	losing
13.	come	comes	came	coming
14.	become	becomes	became	becoming
15.	overcome	overcomes	overcame	overcoming
16.	welcome	welcomes	welcomed	welcoming
17.	* some	something	somebody	somewhere
18.	someway	sometime	sometimes	handsome
19.	room	rooms	roomed	rooming
20.	broom	brooms	* roomer	roomers
21.	broomstick	broomsticks	* rumor	rumors
22.	groom	grooms	groomed	grooming
23.	boom	booms	boomed	booming
24.	loom	looms	loomed	looming
25.	bloom	blooms	bloomed	blooming

* Homophones:

tease / tees / teas   It's fun to tease Tom about his golf tees and his herbal teas.
some / sum   Do some of you know how to sum up a story?
rumor / roomer   Who started the rumor about the new boarding house roomer.

The complete -ease family is found on p. 435 in TPES; the -ooze, p. 435; -ome ("UM") p. 334, -oom, p. 418.

Evaluation Test #4 (After 160 Days)

		Pattern being tested	Lesson word is in
1.	Only a pig takes up two parking sp**aces**.	aces	122
2.	His only adv**ice** was to be true to yourself.	ice	123
3.	There are too many g**angs** in our neighborhood.	angs	122
4.	How many ch**anges** do you want to make?	anges	126
5.	Who was that str**anger** wearing the mask?	anger	126
6.	I hate to hear about someone getting m**ugged**.	ugged	131
7.	I hope you're just k**idding** me.	idding	132
8.	My sister is always h**iding** her things from me.	iding	136
9.	It g**oes** with the territory.	oes	142
10.	One hundred is just one with two zer**oes** after it.	oes	142
11.	Sarah says she d**oesn't** ever want to get married.	oesn't	147
12.	We were not all**owed** to go.	owed	151
13.	They are sl**owing** down.	owing	148
14.	We'll be back after the foll**owing**.	owing	152
15.	Will you pl**ease** close the door behind you.	ease	153
16.	I enjoy eating shr**edded** wheat for breakfast.	edded	155
17.	I enjoy taking a sn**ooze** right after supper.	ooze	157
18.	I love to see the flowers in bl**oom**.	oom	157
19.	What on **earth** are you talking about?	earth	161
20.	What day is your b**irth**day?	irth	163

Name_____   Date_____

Evaluation Test #4

1. Only a pig takes up two parking sp_____.

2. His only adv_____ was to be true to yourself.

3. There are too many g_____ in our neighborhood.

4. How many ch_____ do you want to make?

5. Who was that str_____ wearing the mask?

6. I hate to hear about someone getting m_____.

7. I hope you're just k_____ me.

8. My sister is always h_____ her things from me.

9. It g_____ with the territory.

10. One hundred is just one with two zer_____ after it.

11. Sarah says she d_____ ever want to get married.

12. We were not all_____ to go.

13. They are sl_____ down.

14. We'll be back after the foll_____.

15. Will you pl_____ close the door behind you.

16. I enjoy eating shr_____ wheat for breakfast.

17. I enjoy taking a sn_____ right after supper.

18. I love to see the flowers in bl_____ .

19. What on_____are you talking about?

20. What day is your b_____day?

	161st day	162nd day	163rd day	164th day
1.	**earth**	earths	Eartha Kitt	unearthly
2.	unearth	unearths	unearthed	unearthing
3.	* **birth**	births	**birthday**	birthdays
4.	* **berth**	berths	Bertha	smooth
5.	**tooth**	**teeth**	toothbrush	smoothly
6.	booth	booths	sawtooth	tollbooth
7.	Ruth	Ruth's tooth	truth	truth
8.	truth	truths	truthful	truthfully
9.	you	youth	youthful	youthfulness
10.	soothe	soothes	soothed	soothing
11.	smooth	smoothes	smoothed	smoothing
12.	**both**	**both**	**both**	**both**
13.	**breathe**	breathes	breathed	**breathing**
14.	**breath**	breaths	breathless	breathlessly
15.	**death**	deaths	**death**	deaths
16.	badge	badges	Madge	Madge's badges
17.	badger	badgers	badgers	badgering
18.	**edge**	edges	edged	edging
19.	ledge	ledges	edger	edgers
20.	pledge	pledges	pledged	pledging
21.	hedge	hedges	hedged	hedging
22.	wedge	wedges	wedged	wedging
23.	sledge	sledges	acknowledges	acknowledging
24.	dredge	dredges	dredged	dredging
25.	knowledge	acknowledge	acknowledged	**acknowledgment**

* Homophones:

birth	1991 saw the birth of a new Russia.
berth	I got a lower berth to sleep in on the train.

See the complete -rth family on p. 515 in *The Patterns of English Spelling* (TPES), the -ooth, p. 277; -oth, p. 277; -eath, p. 275; -eathe, p. 279; -edge, p. 212.

165th day	166th day	167th day	168th day
1. dodge	dodges	dodged	dodging
2. dodger	dodgers	lodger	lodgers
3. lodge	lodges	lodged	lodging
4. dislodge	dislodges	dislodged	dislodging
5. * lie	* lies	lied	lying
6. * die	* dies	* died	* dying
7. * dye	* dyes	* dyed	* dyeing
8. * pie	pies	(fi **fie** foe fum)	doesn't
9. vie	vies	vied	vying
10. tie	ties	* tied	tying
11. * eye	eyes	eyed	eying
12. * lye	lyes	* aye	* ayes
13. * bye	byes	goodbye	goodbyes
14. * by	goodby	good-by	good-bye
15. rye	buckeye	walleye	redeye
16. Popeye	pinkeye	blue-eyed	brown-eyed
17. cry	cries	cried	crying
18. dry	dries	dried	drying
19. fry	fries	fried	frying
20. pry	* pries	* pried	prying
21. try	tries	tried	trying
22. sky	skies	sly	my, oh my
23. thereby	whereby	slyly	when
24. fly	flies	spry	flying
25. why	who	what	where

* Homophones:

lie / lye — It's a sin to tell a lie. Lye is often used to unplug drains.
die / dye — I want to die when I'm 175. My wife wants to dye her hair red at 125.
pie / pi — Would you like a piece of pie? The value of pi is 3.14159....
tied / tide — He was all tied up with rope. The ship sailed as the tide started to go out.
eye / aye / I — Keep an eye out for strangers. Aye, aye sir. I sure will, sir.
by / buy / bye — By the way, did he try to buy a bye for the first round of the tournament?
pries / prize — She pries into everything. She won first prize for snoopiness.
pried / pride — Pandora pried open the box. We all should take pride in our work.
See the complete -odge family on p. 212 in TPES; -ie & -ye & -y, p. 308.

	169th day	170th day	171st day	172nd day
1.	spy	spies	spied	spying
2.	ply	plies	plied	plying
3.	apply	applies	applied	applying
4.	supply	**supplies**	supplied	supplying
5.	comply	complies	complied	complying
6.	multiply	multiplies	multiplied	multiplying
7.	reply	replies	replied	replying
8.	**rely**	**relies**	**relied**	**relying**
9.	occupy	occupies	occupied	occupying
10.	satisfy	satisfies	satisfied	satisfying
11.	dissatisfy	dissatisfies	dissatisfied	dissatisfying
12.	horrify	horrifies	horrified	horrifying
13.	terrify	terrifies	terrified	terrifying
14.	solidify	solidifies	solidified	solidifying
15.	falsify	falsifies	falsified	falsifying
16.	deny	denies	denied	denying
17.	ally	allies	allied	allying
18.	July	July's days	lullaby	lullabies
19.	inning	innings	**could**	**couldn't**
20	winning	winnings	**should**	**shouldn't**
21.	**beginning**	beginnings	*** would**	**wouldn't**
22.	spinner	spinners	**school**	schools
23.	He isn't the one.	It's too bad.	She doesn't know.	He won't know.
24.	She wasn't here.	He hasn't got it.	They didn't get it.	We don't care.
25.	We were there.	We weren't here.	Where were they?	He can't go.

* Homophones:

wood   The box was made out of wood, pine I think.
would   Would you please follow directions?

The complete -y family is found on pp. 307, 308, & 715 in *The Patterns of English Spelling* (TPES); -nner, p. 635.

66

	173rd day	174th day	175th day	176th day
1.	**that**	**isn't**	**wasn't**	**weren't**
2.	batter	batters	battery	batteries
3.	shatter	shatters	shattered	shattering
4.	scatter	scatters	scattered	scattering
5.	flatter	flatters	flattered	flattering
6.	spatter	spatters	spattered	spattering
7.	**show**	shows	showed	showing
8.	*** boy**	boys	**toy**	toys
9.	annoy	annoys	annoyed	annoying
10.	enjoy	enjoys	enjoyed	enjoying
11.	employ	employs	employed	employing
12.	oak	oaks	haven't	hasn't
13.	soak	soaks	soaked	soaking
14.	*** coal**	coals	goal	goals
15.	*** bowl**	bowls	bowled	bowling
16.	bowler	bowlers	**won't**	**don't**
17.	*** roll**	rolls	rolled	rolling
18.	troll	trolls	trolled	trolling
19.	stroll	strolls	strolled	strolling
20.	**soap**	soaps	soaped	soaping
21.	give	gives	gave/given	giving
22.	forgive	forgives	forgave	forgiving
23.	live	lives	lived	living
24.	liver	giver	sliver	slivers
25.	deliver	delivers	delivered	delivering

* Homophones:

boy	Why is it that we can say, "Oh boy, it's a girl!" but never, "Oh girl, it's a boy!"?
buoy	They use a buoy to mark places like shipping lanes in rivers.
coal	They mine a lot of coal near Newcastle.
Cole	Was Ol' King Cole really a merry ol' soul?
boll / bowl	A boll weevil can never bowl a 300 game.
roll	Just roll the ball. Don't throw it.
role	Did you get the leading role in the play?

The complete -at family is found on p. 131, the -atter, p. 637; -oy, p. 303; -oak, p. 409, -oal, p. 413, -owl 415; -oll, p. 241; -oap, 425.

	177th day	178th day	179th day	180th day
1.	* band	bands	banded	banding
2.	sand	sands	sanded	sanding
3.	bend	bends	bent	bending
4.	spend	spends	spent	spending
5.	bite	bites	white	kite
6.	save	saves	saved	saving
7.	brave	braves	braved	braving
8.	have	has	having	haven't
9.	spill	spills	drill	drills
10.	skill	skills	skilled	unskilled
11.	will	willing	willingly	willingness
12.	book	books	took	crook
13.	joke	jokes	joked	joking
14.	spoke	spokes	poke	poking
15.	rule	rules	ruled	ruling
16.	wool	year	years	spears
17.	face	faces	faced	facing
18.	race	races	raced	racing
19.	brace	braces	braced	bracing
20.	trace	traces	traced	tracing
21.	chase	chases	chased	chasing
22.	base	bases	based	basing
23.	erase	erases	erased	basic
24.	eraser	erasers	off-base	basically
25.	case	cases	vase	vases

* Homophones:

band   I would like to play in a band.
banned   That book was banned in Boston.

The complete -and family is found on p. 227 in TPES; the -ite, 357; the -ave, p. 324, -ill, p. 151, -ook, p. 409; -oke, p. 329; -ule, p. 331; -ool 416; -ace & -ase p. 343.

Final Evaluation Test

	Pattern being tested	Lesson word is in
1. Let's go back to the very beg**inning**.	inning	5
2. Let's not get into a sh**outing** match.	outing	12
3. I'm pl**anning** on having a good vacation.	anning	20
4. I hate to have spl**itting** headaches.	itting	24
5. My flashlight needs a new b**attery**.	attery	27
6. They are bu**ilding** a new house.	ilding	36
7. It's a very l**oving** puppy.	oving	40
8. The wind was bl**owing** hard.	owing	44
9. We were l**oading** the truck.	oading	48
10. Tom st**ayed** behind to watch the house.	ayed	55
11. He is m**arching** to his own drummer.	arching	60
12. They raise sheep and g**oats**.	oats	64
13. I am dep**ending** upon you.	ending	68
14. He dem**anded** to know who I was.	anded	71
15. The basketball game was really exc**iting**.	iting	76
16. We are h**aving** them over for dinner.	aving	84
17. He rec**alls** how it was when he was a kid.	alls	86
18. Put the package up on the sh**elf**.	elf	89
19. I love the thr**ills** and the sp**ills**.	ills	94 & 90
20. Never carry a conc**ealed** weapon.	ealed	103
21. The pr**ices** remained the same all day.	ices	122
22. We just ch**anged** the oil last week.	anged	127
23. The car sk**idded** to a stop.	idded	131
24. We went on a gu**ided** tour.	ided	143
25. We were not all**owed** to go in early.	owed	151

Name_____   Date_____

Final Evaluation Test

1. Let's go back to the very beg_____.

2. Let's not get into a sh_____ match.

3. I'm pl_____ on having a good vacation.

4. I hate to have spl_____ headaches.

5. My flashlight needs a new b_____ .

6. They are bu_____ a new house.

7. It's a very l_____ puppy.

8. The wind was bl_____ hard.

9. We were l_____ the truck.

10. Tom st_____ behind to watch the house.

11. He is m_____ to his own drummer.

12. They raise sheep and g_____ .

13. I am dep_____ upon you.

14. He dem_____ to know who I was.

15. The basketball game was really exc_____ .

16. We are h_____ them over for dinner.

17. He rec_____ how it was when he was a kid.

18. Put the package up on the sh_____ .

19. I love the thr_____ and the sp_____ .

20. Never carry a conc_____ weapon.

21. The pr_____ remained the same all day.

22. We just ch_____ the oil last week.

23. The car sk_____ to a stop.

24. We went on a gu_____ tour.

25. We were not all_____ to go in early.